Amazing
CITYSCAPES

igloobooks

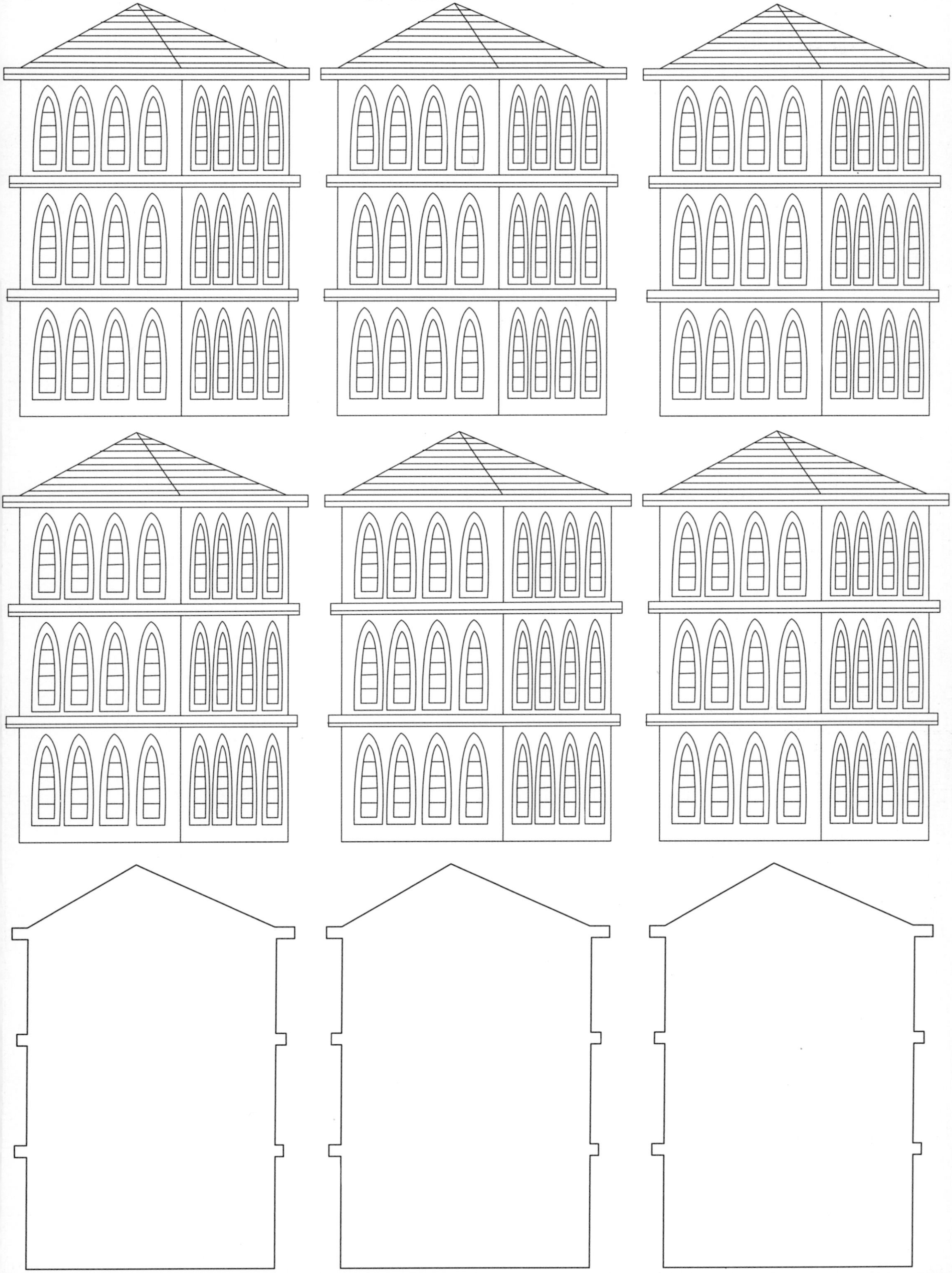

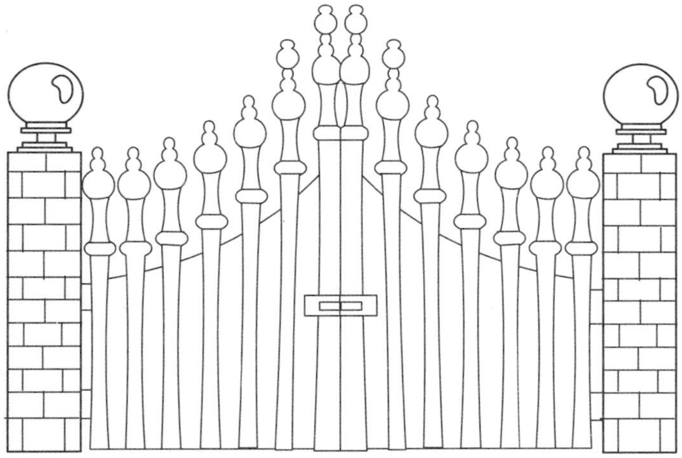
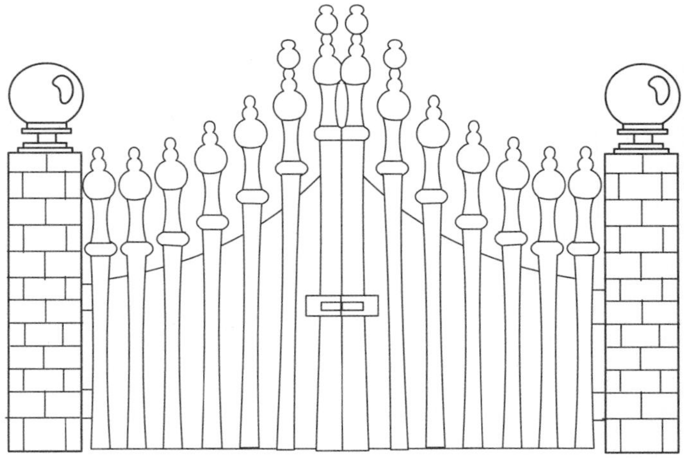
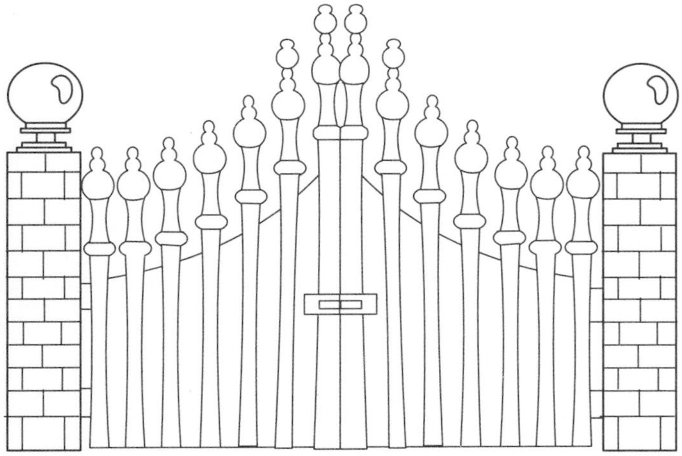
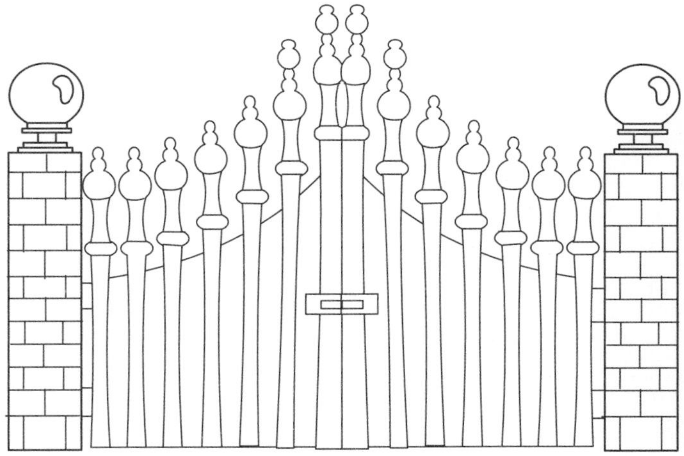
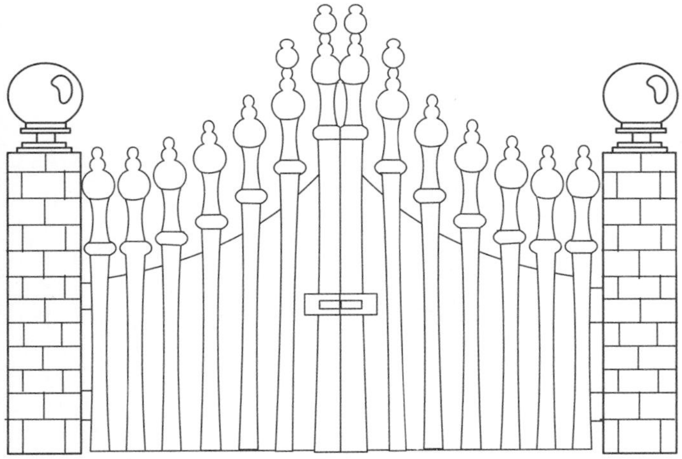
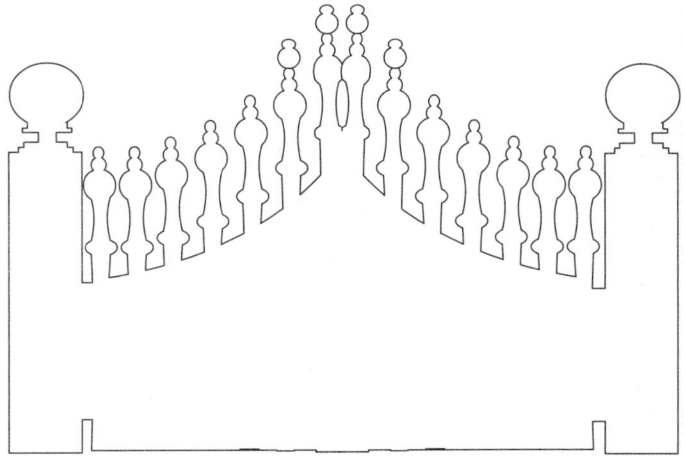

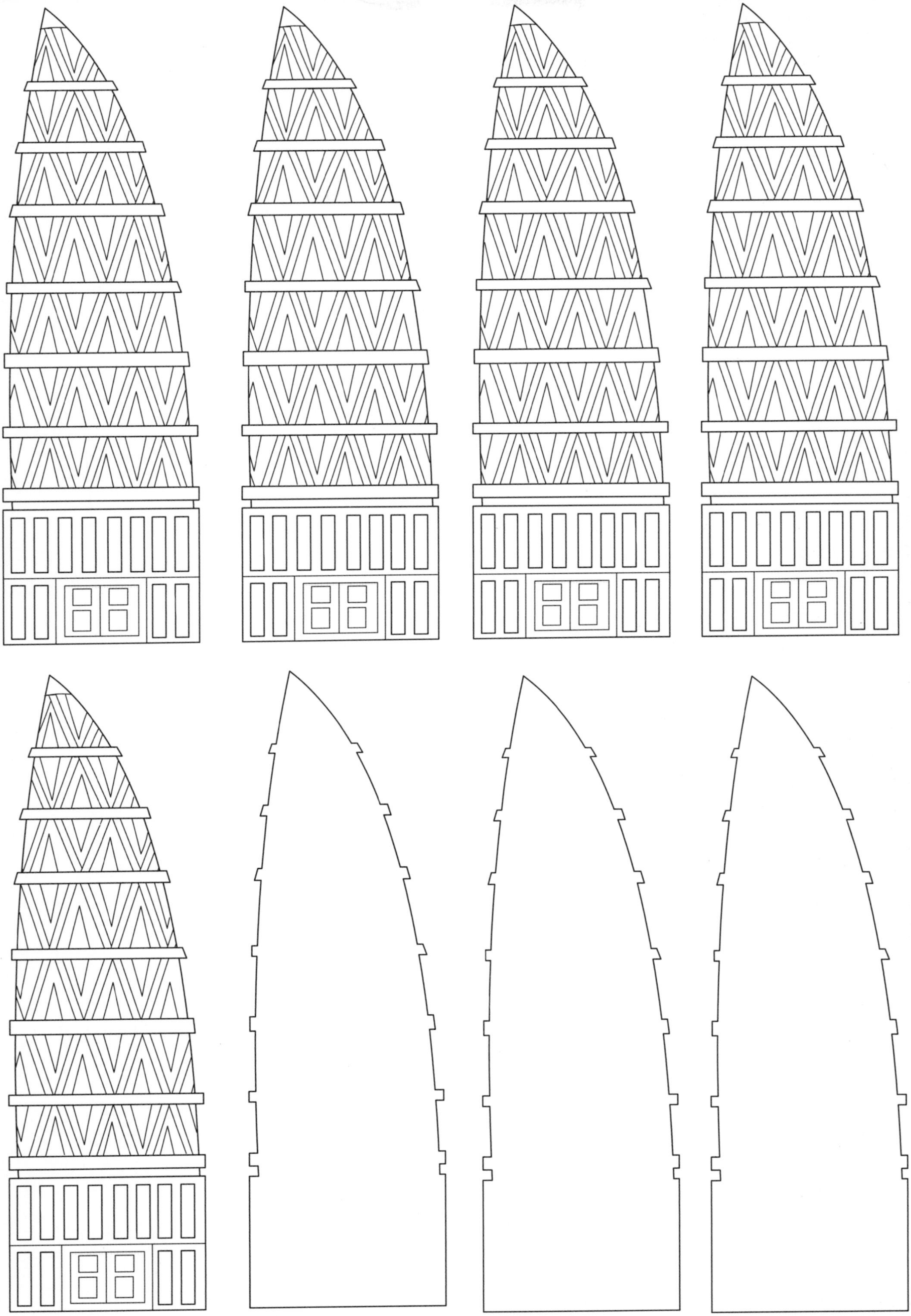

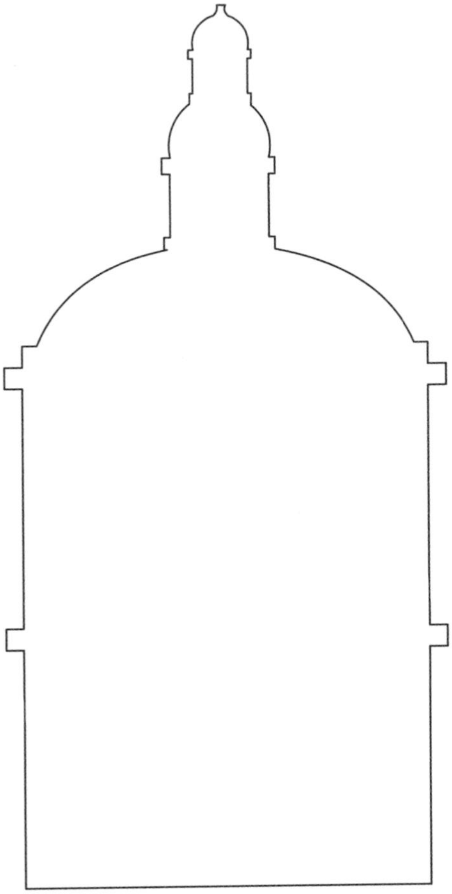
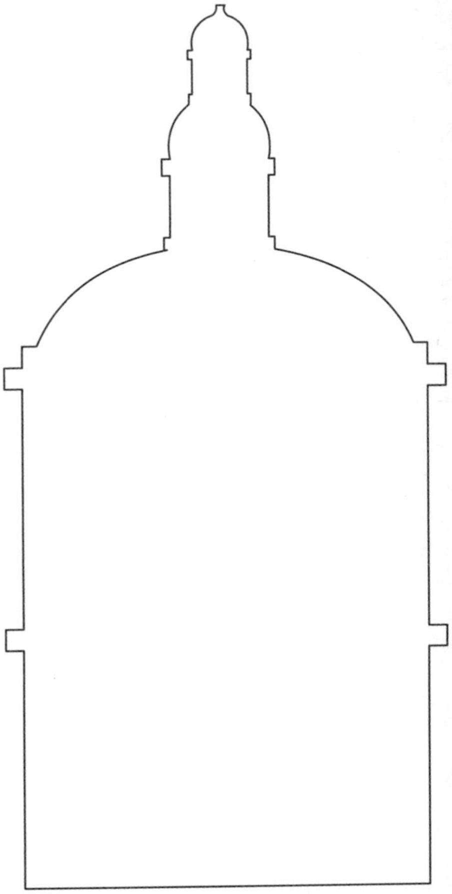

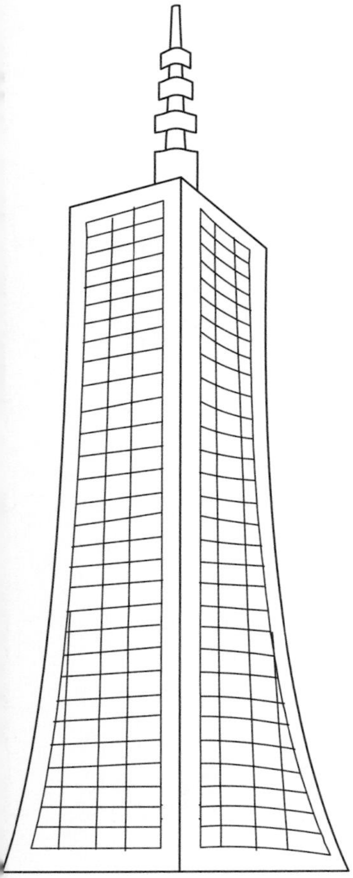
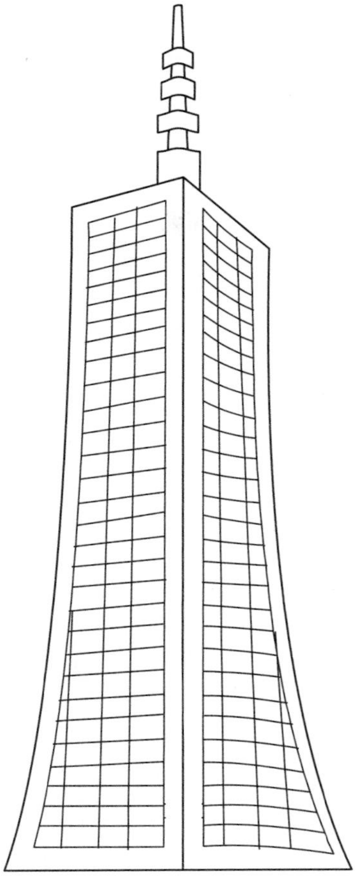
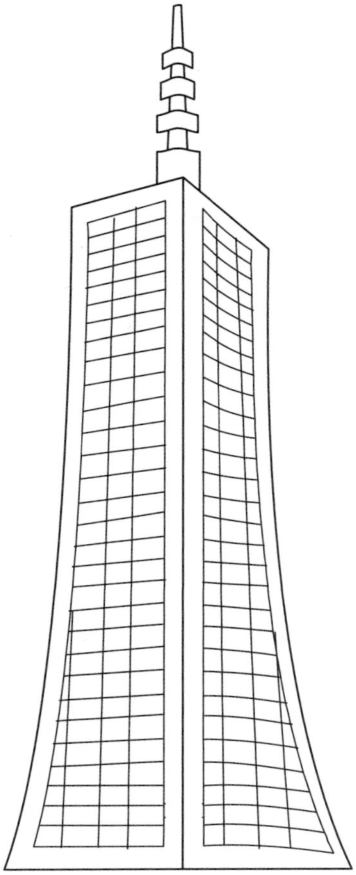
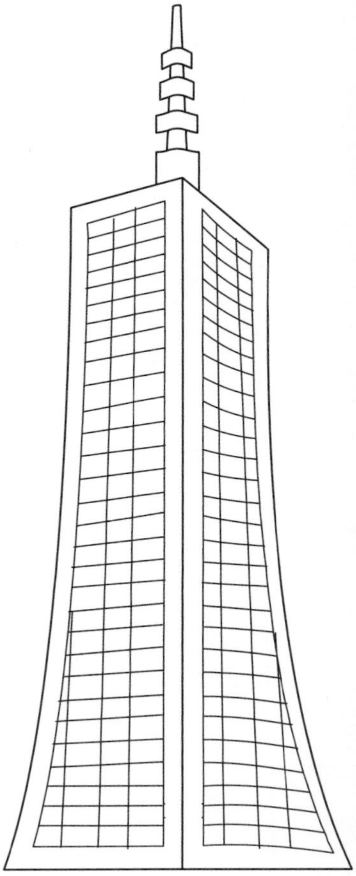
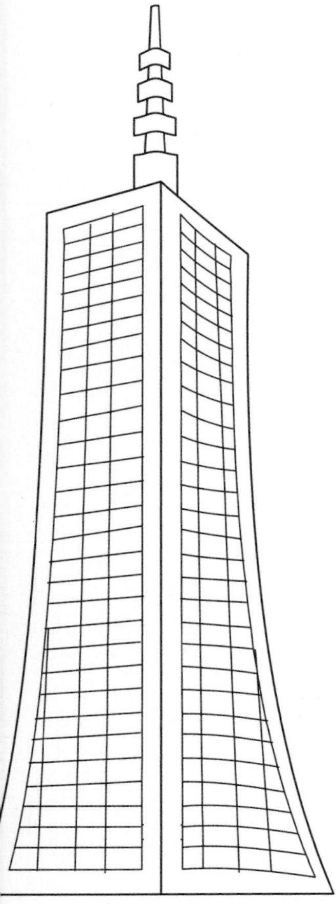
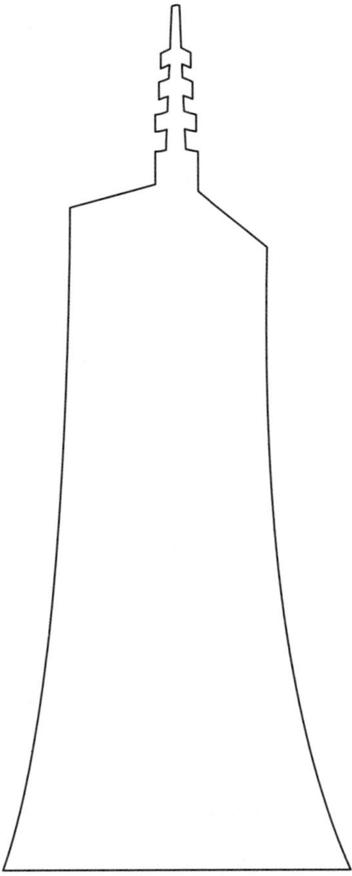
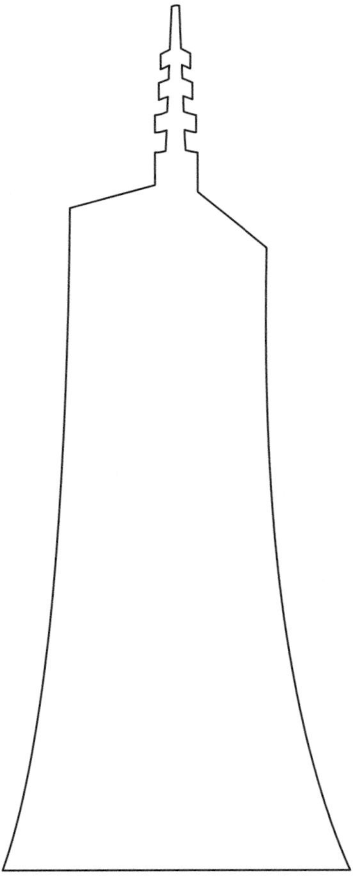
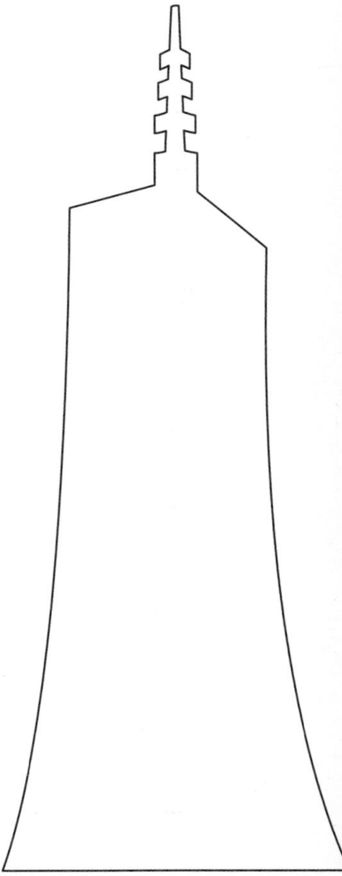

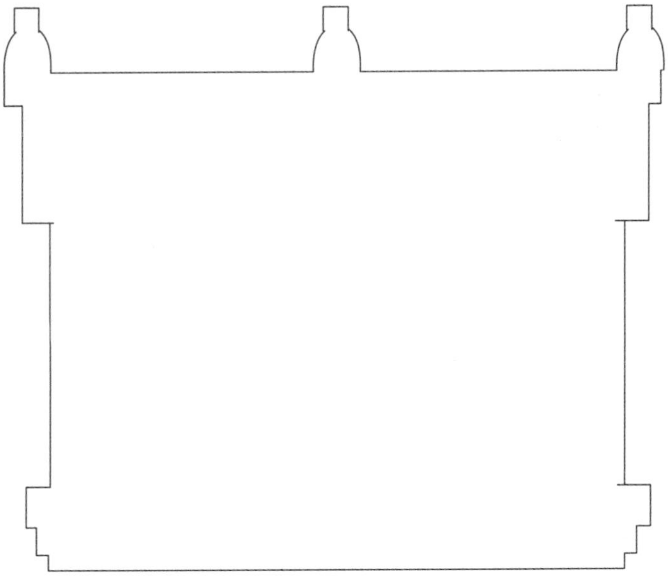
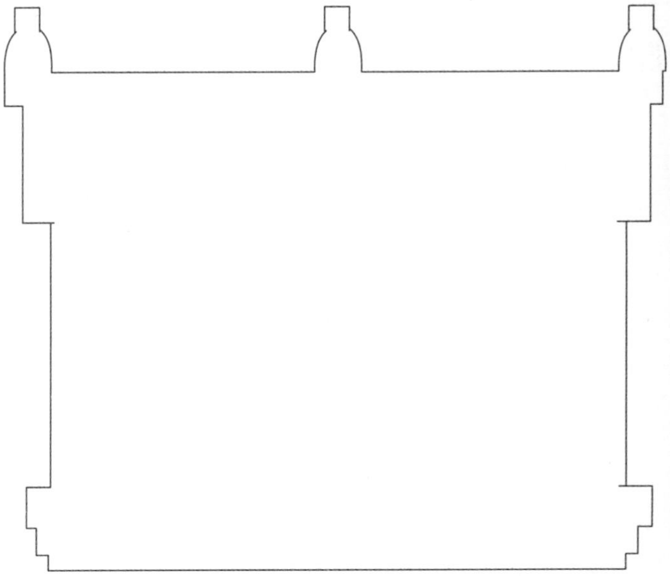

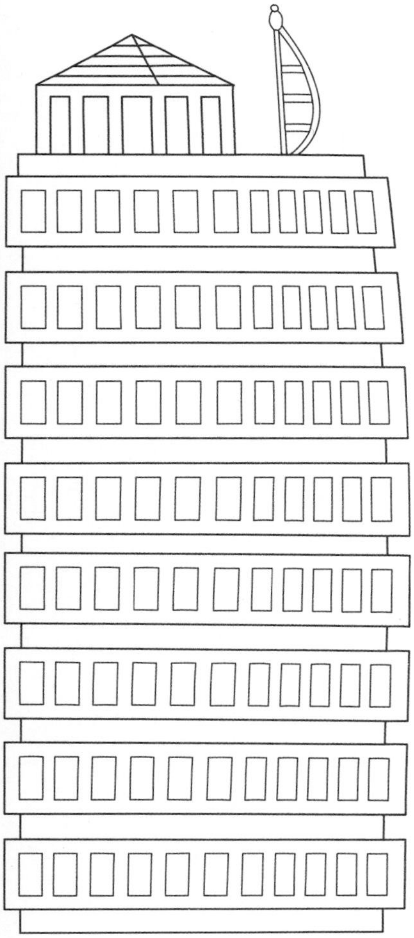
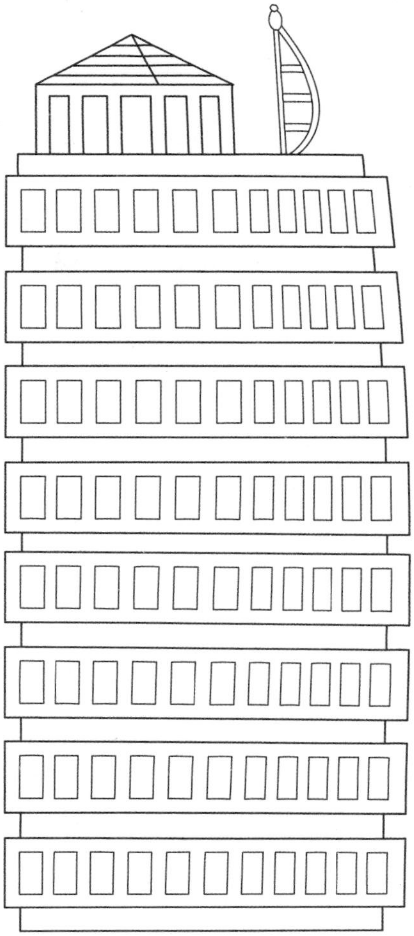

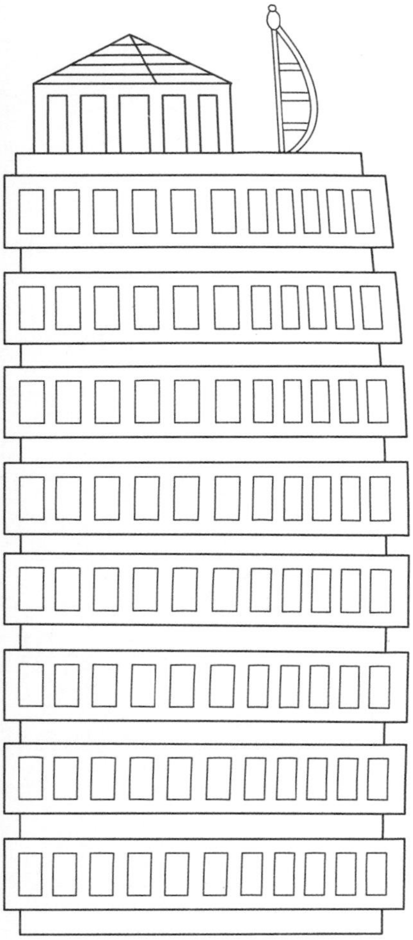
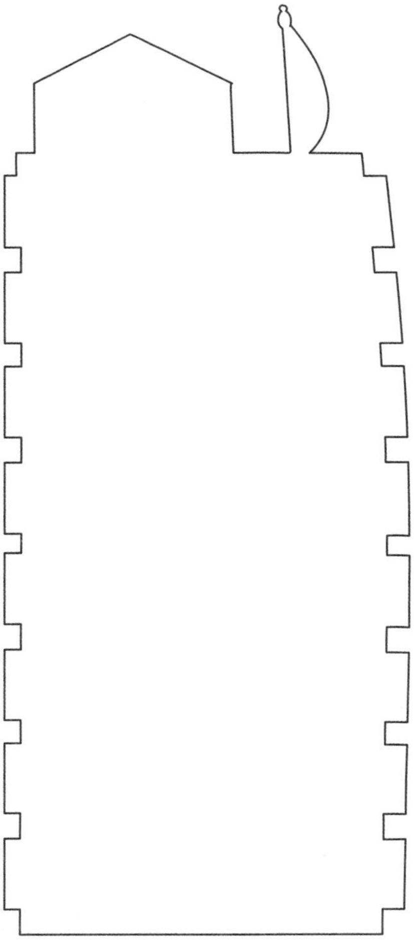
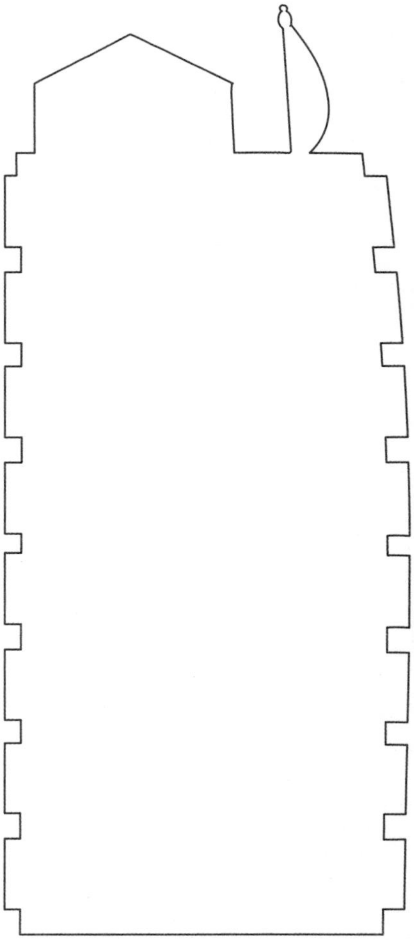

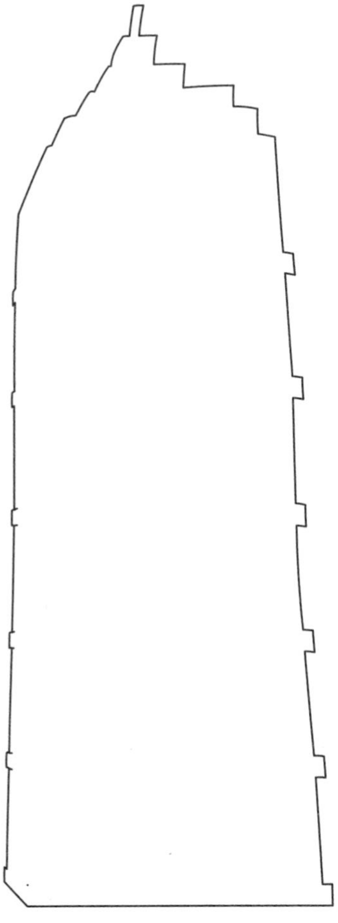
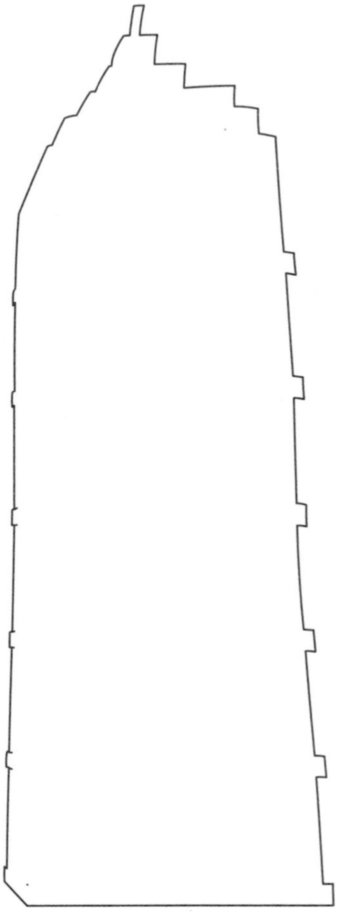
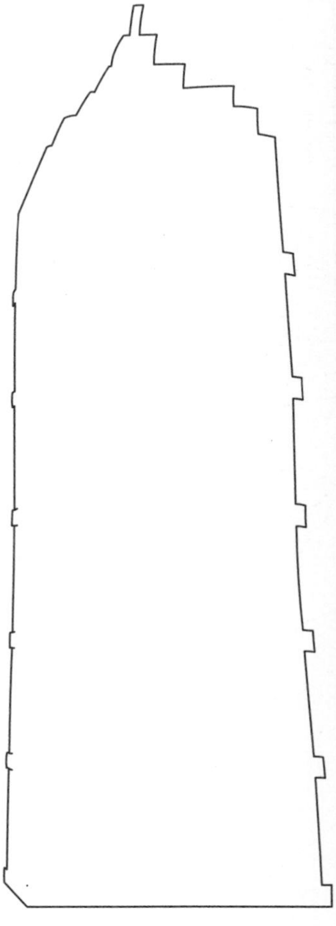

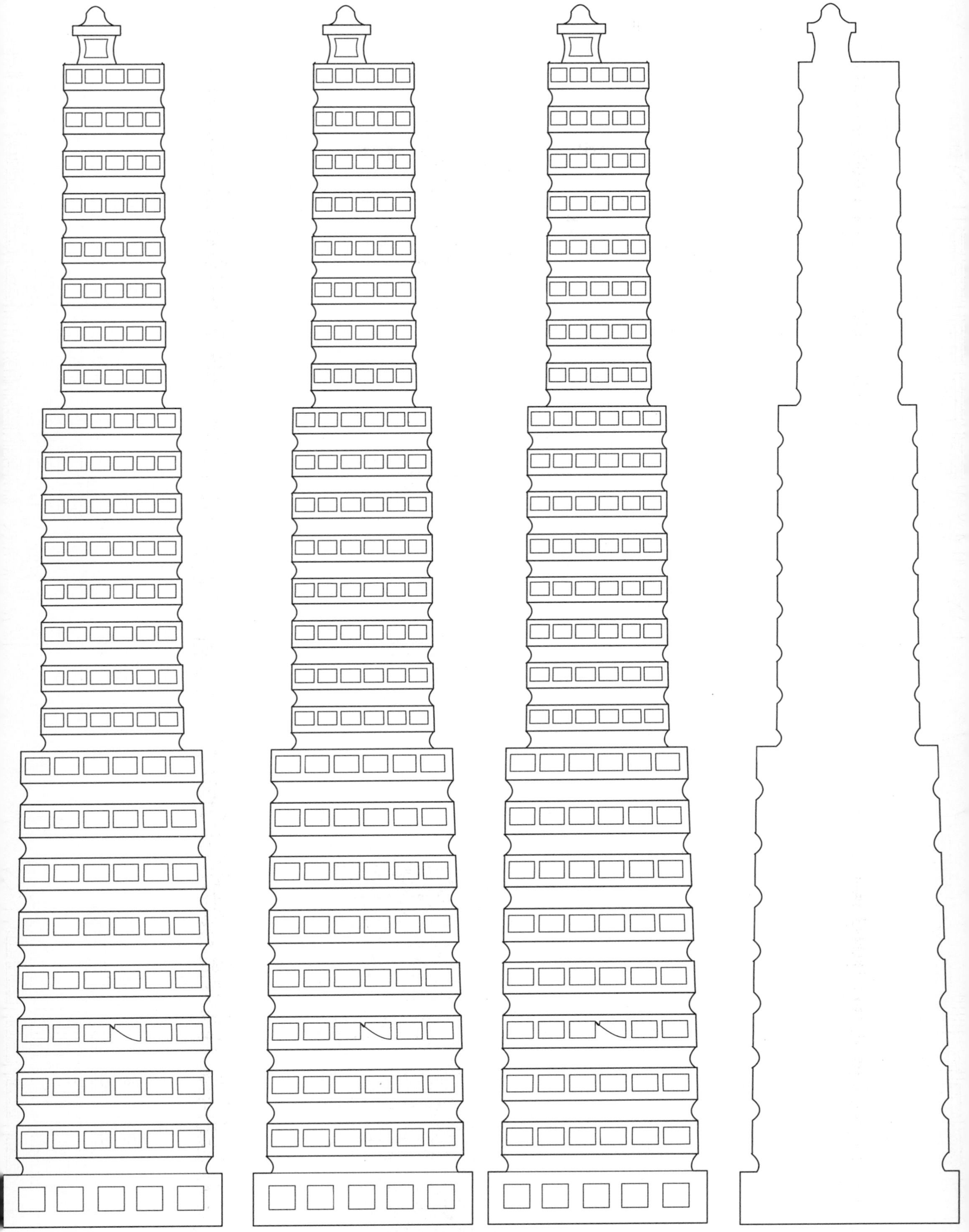

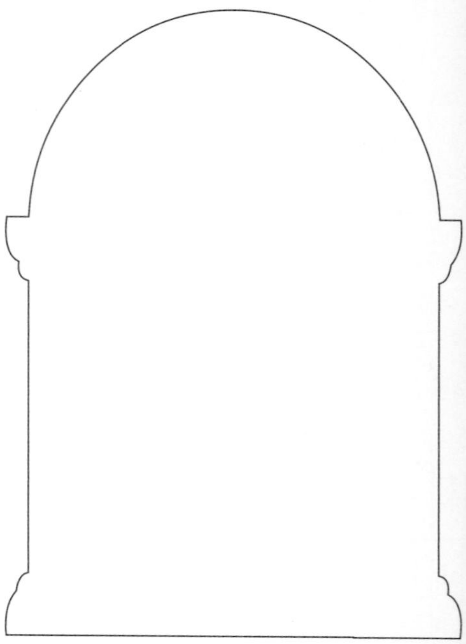

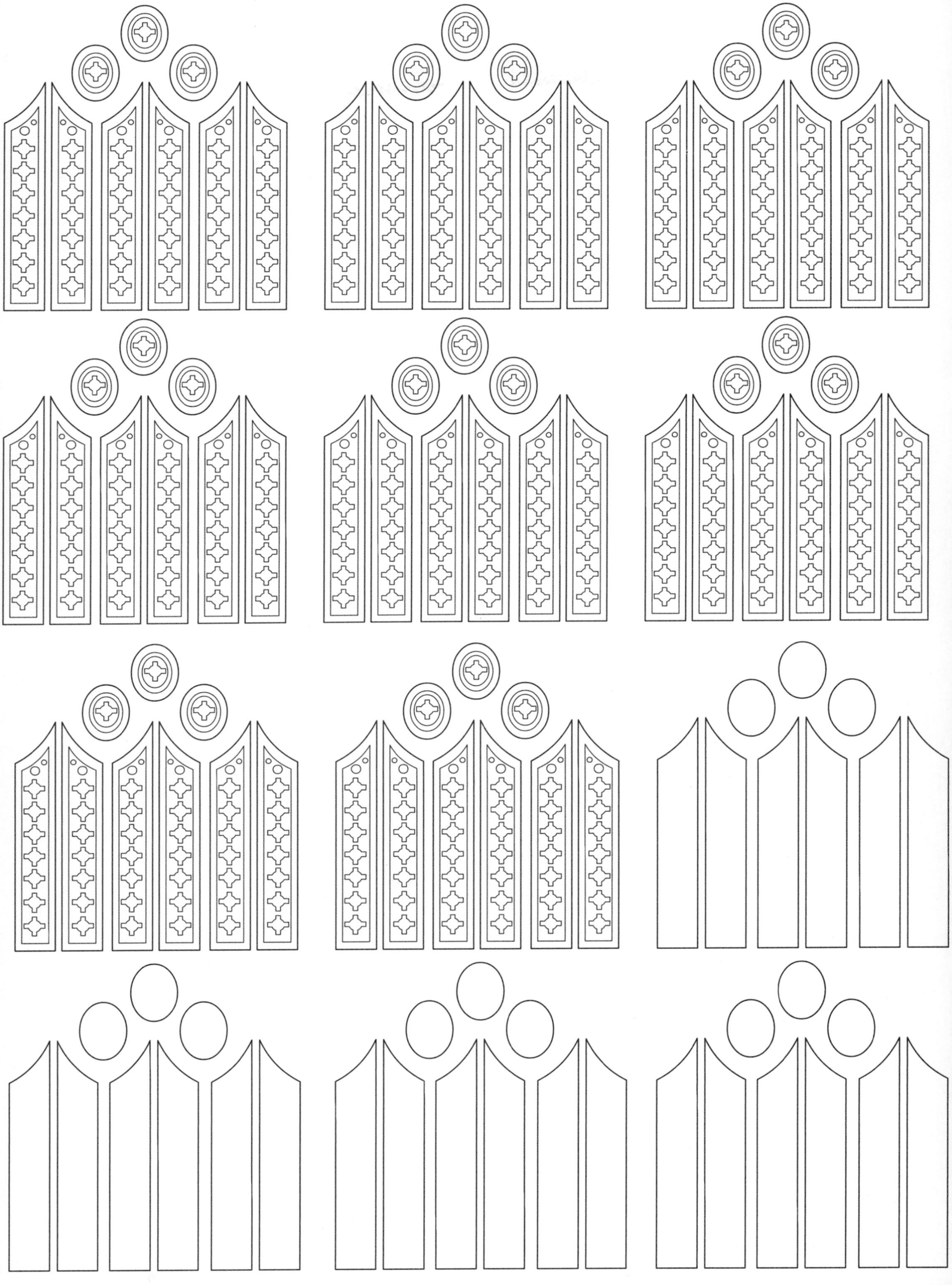

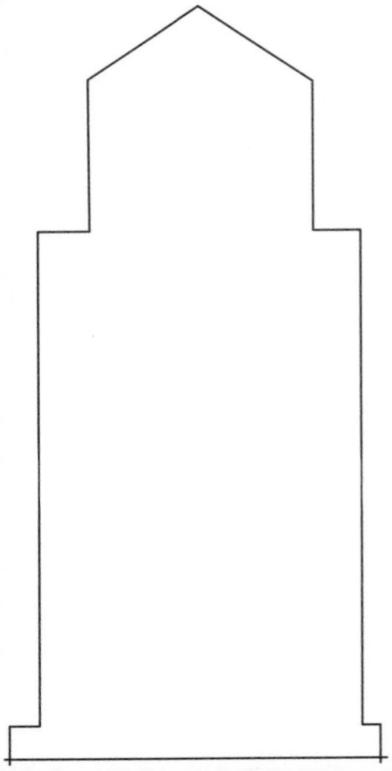
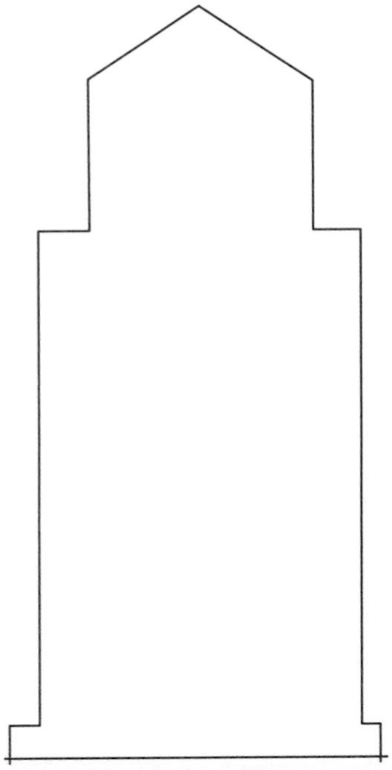
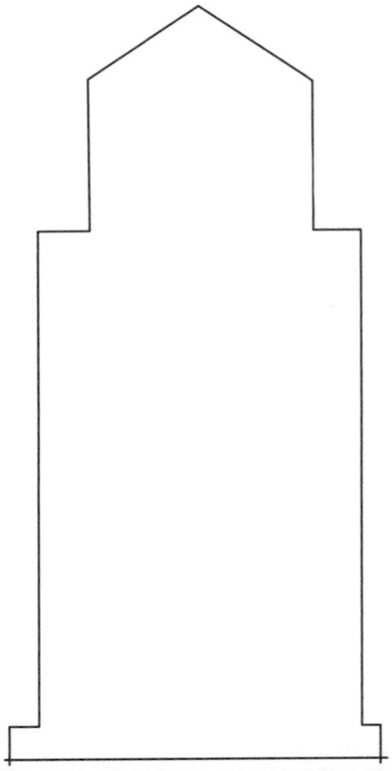
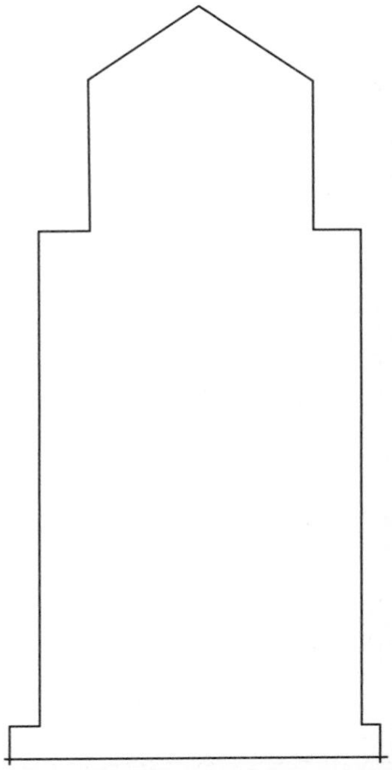

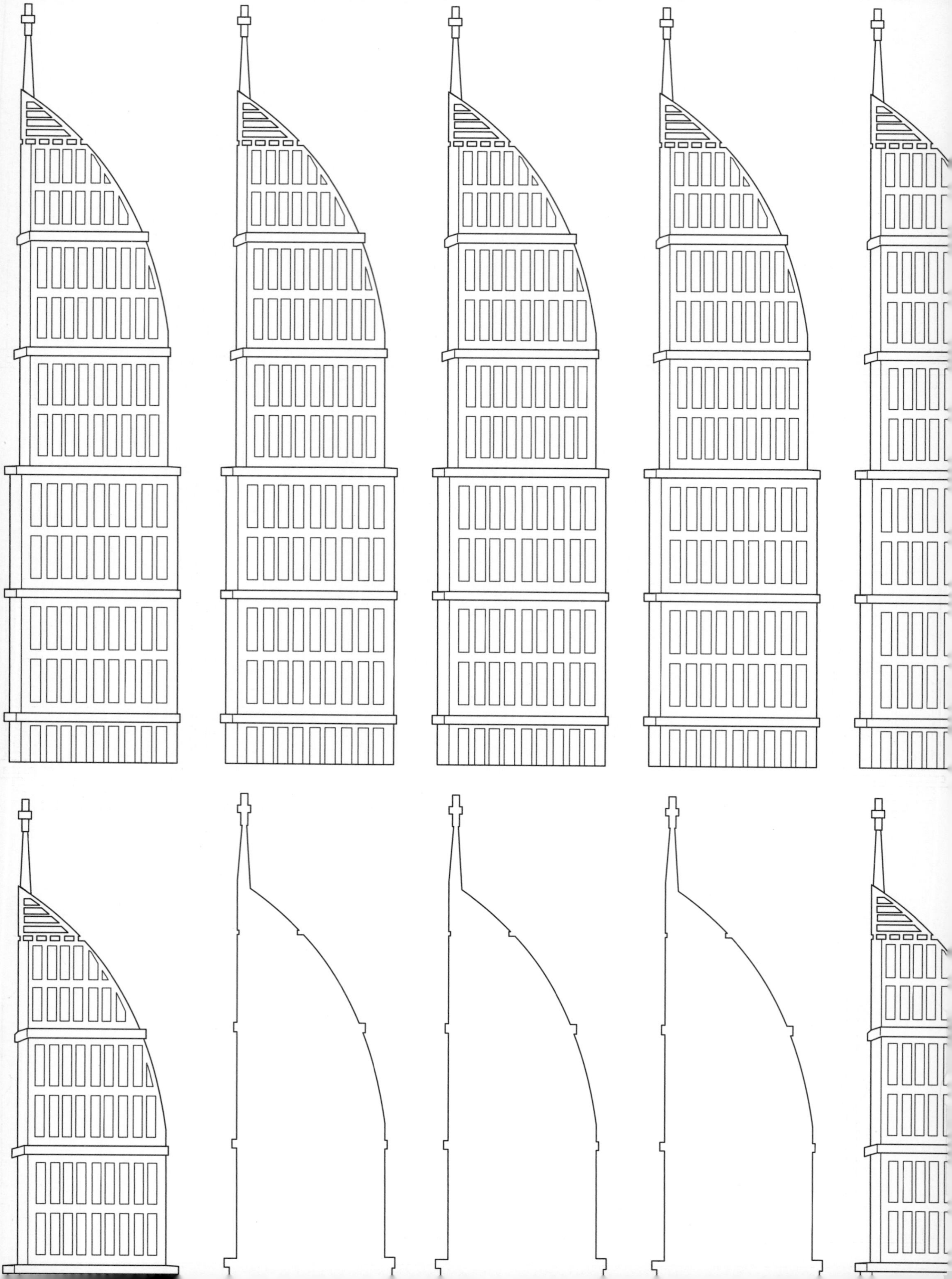

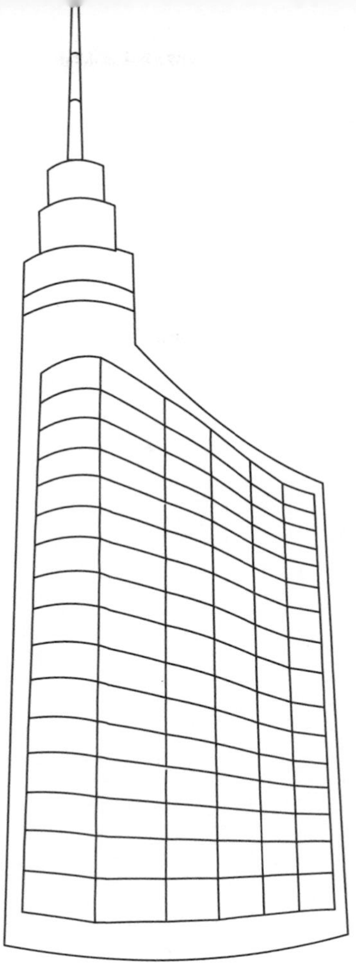
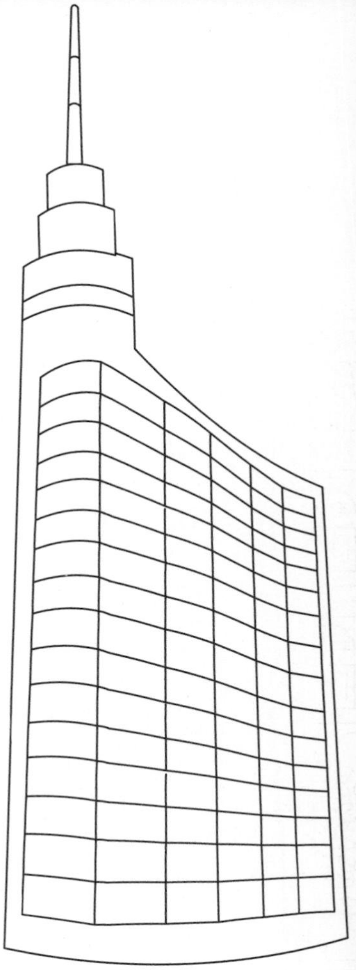

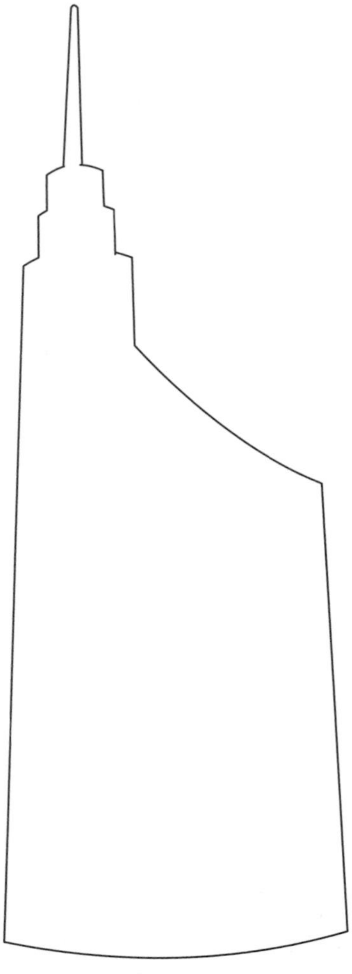
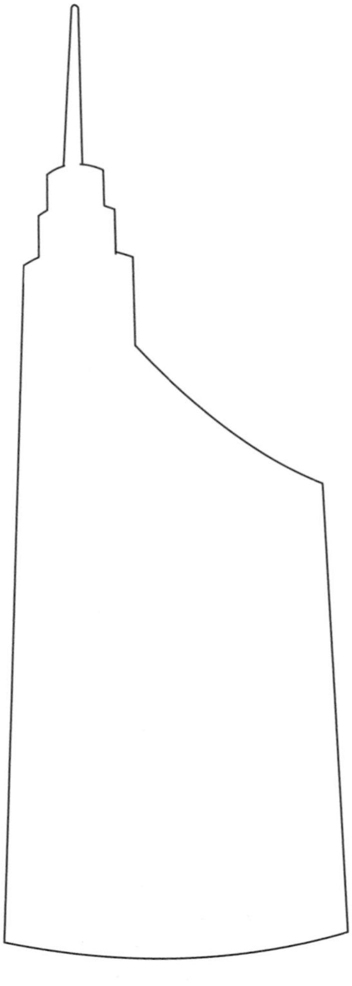
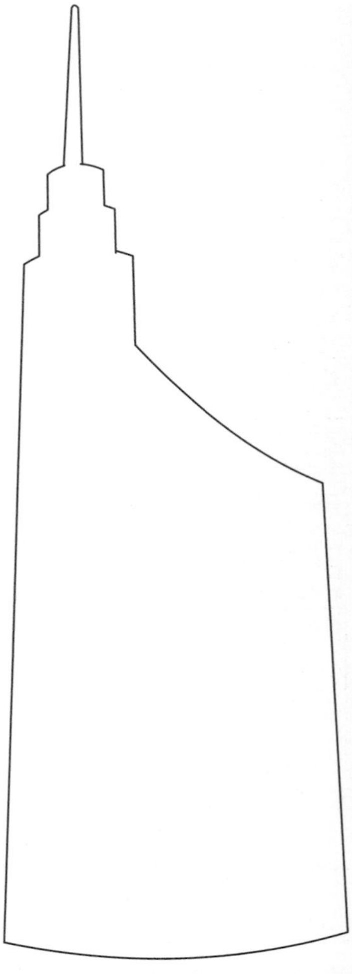

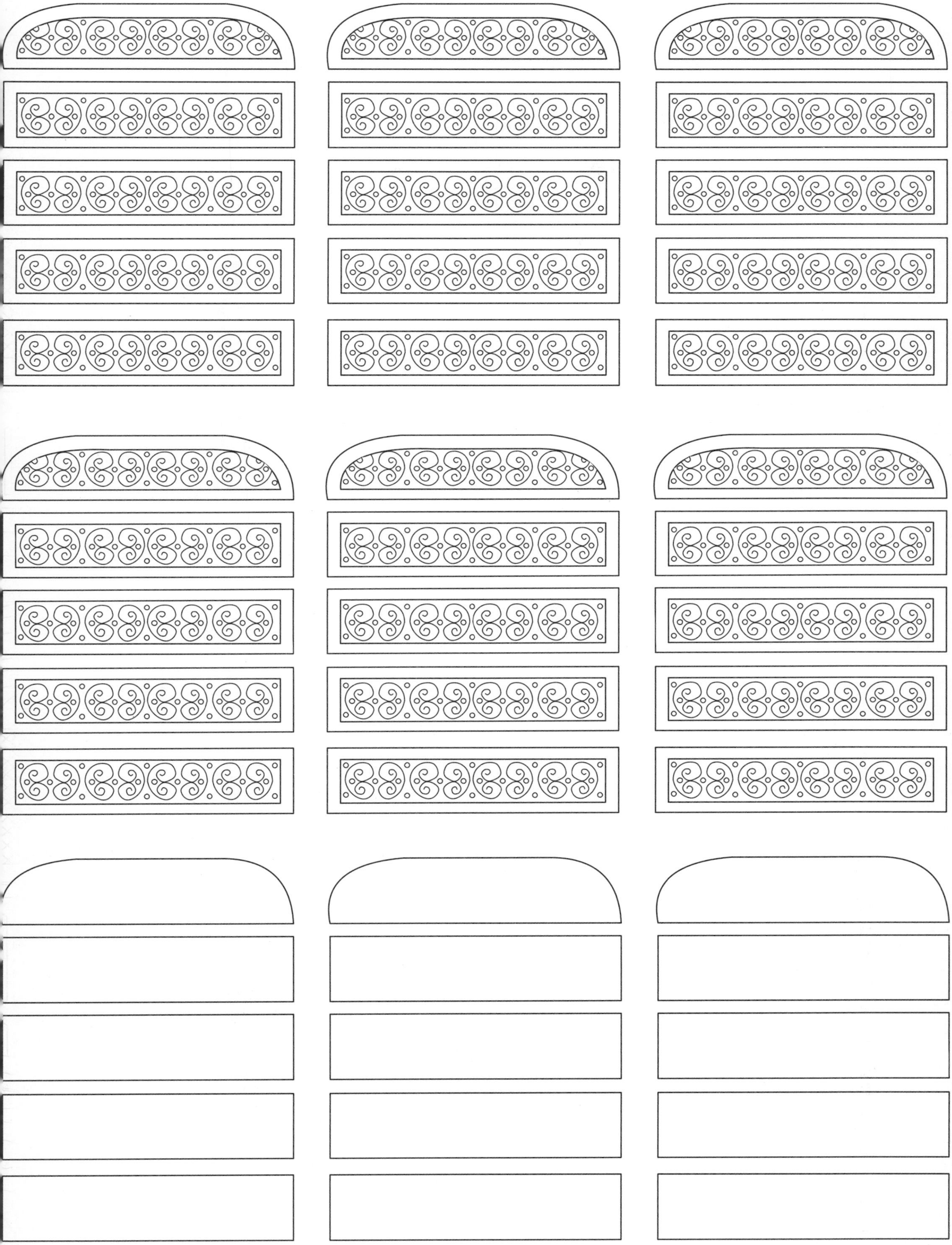

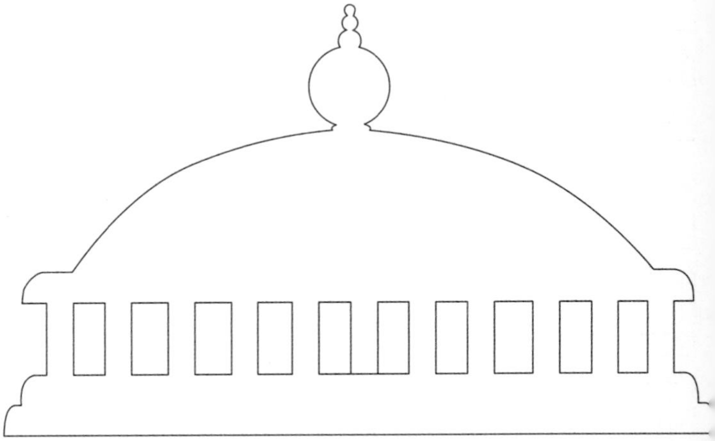
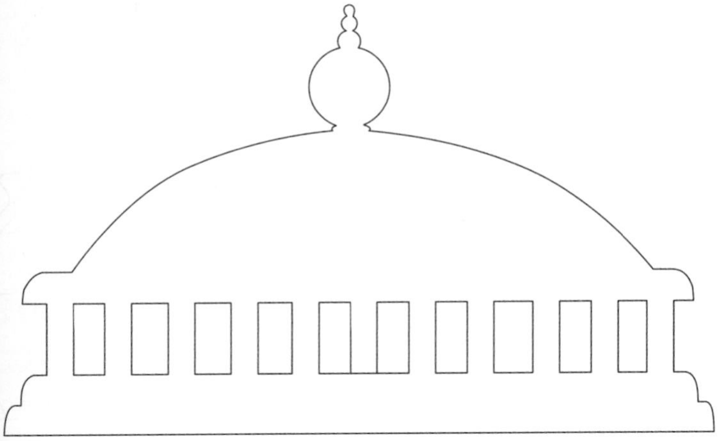
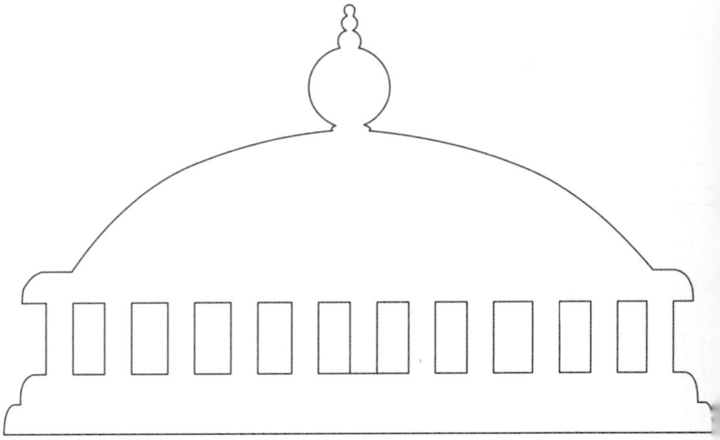

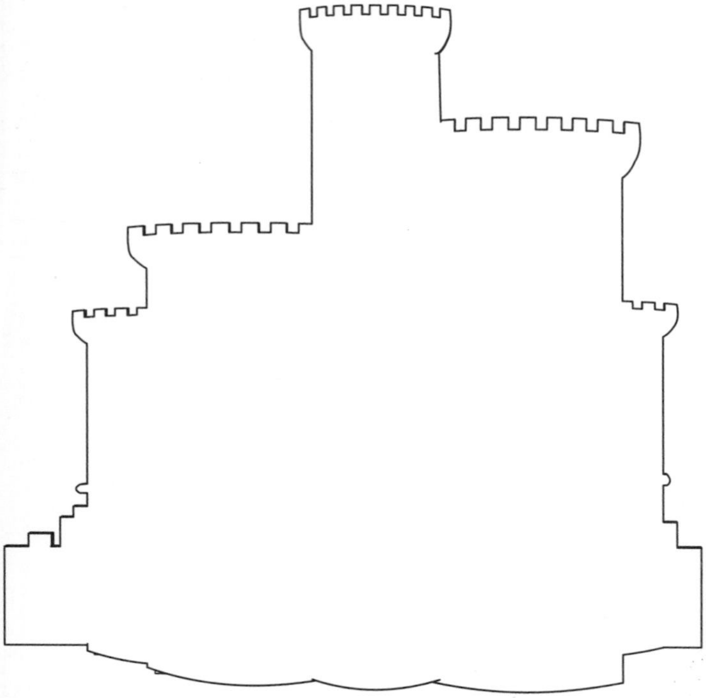

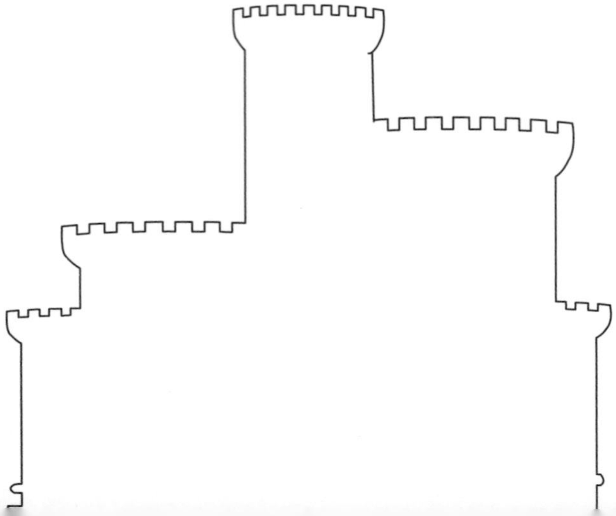
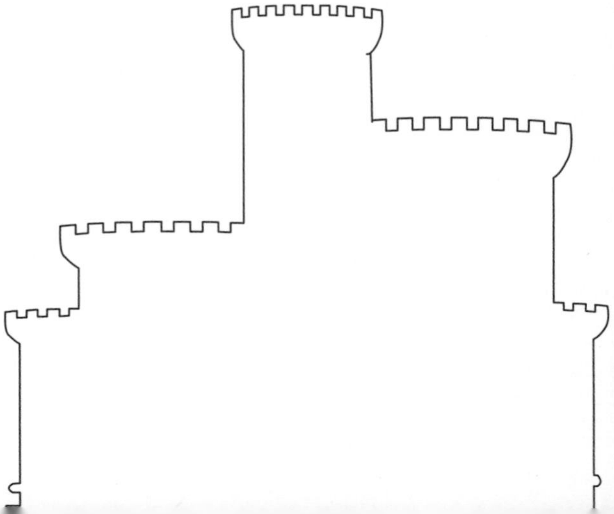

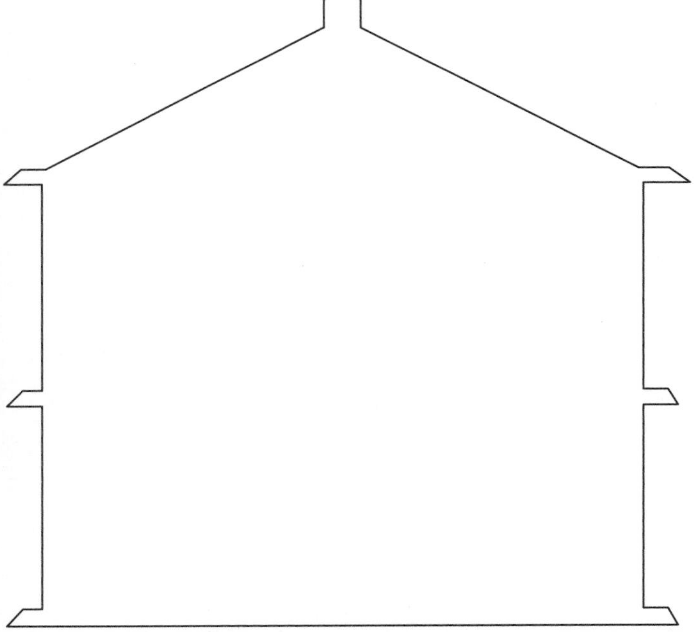
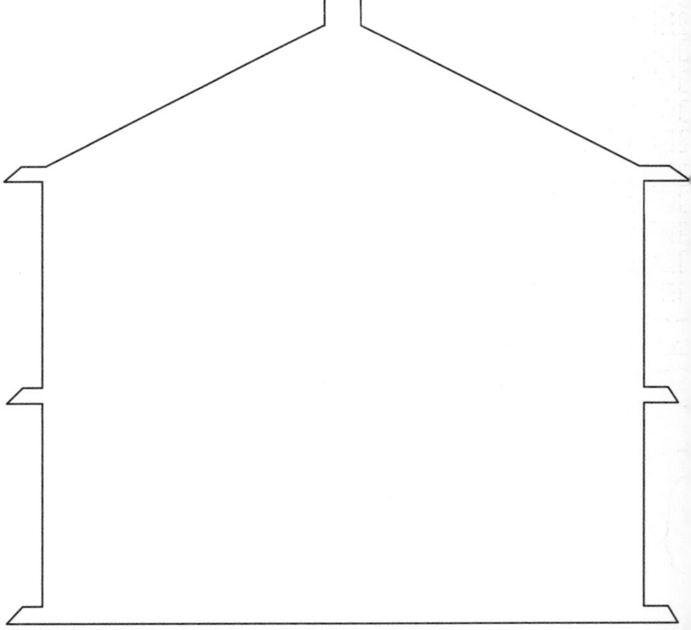

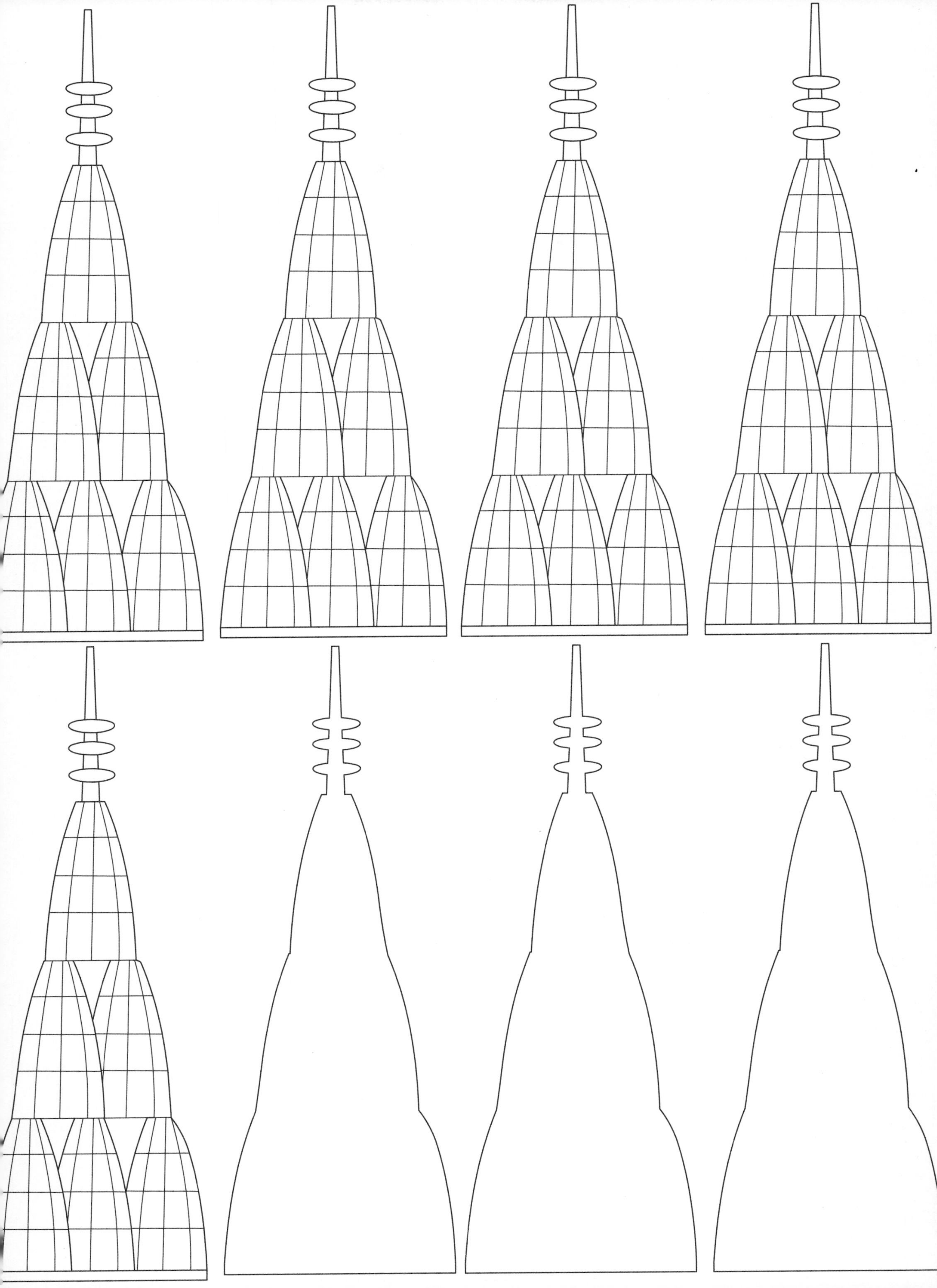

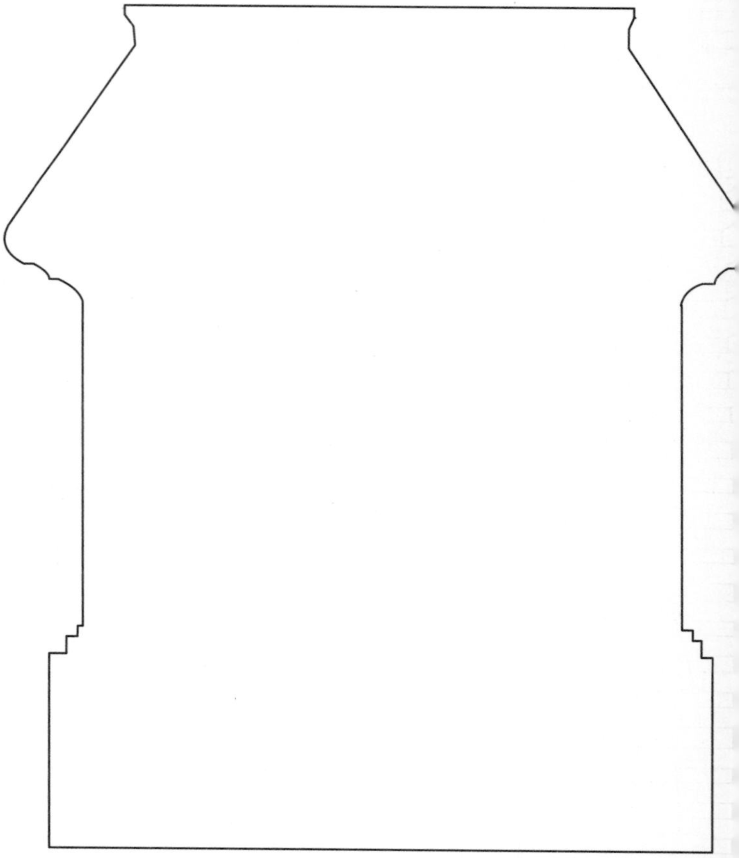
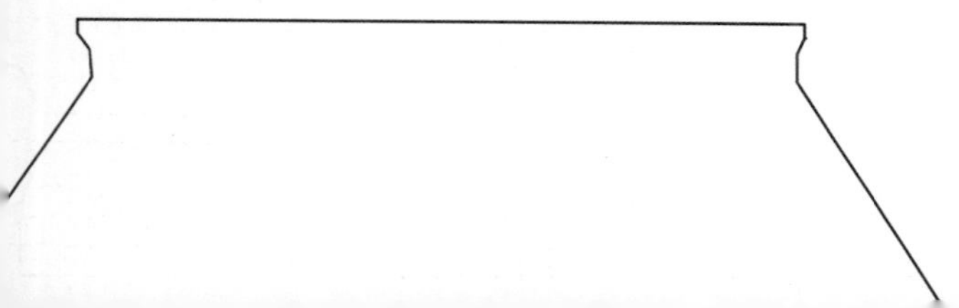
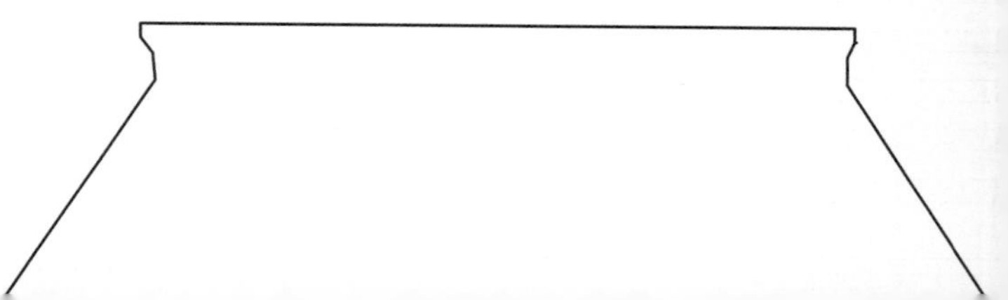

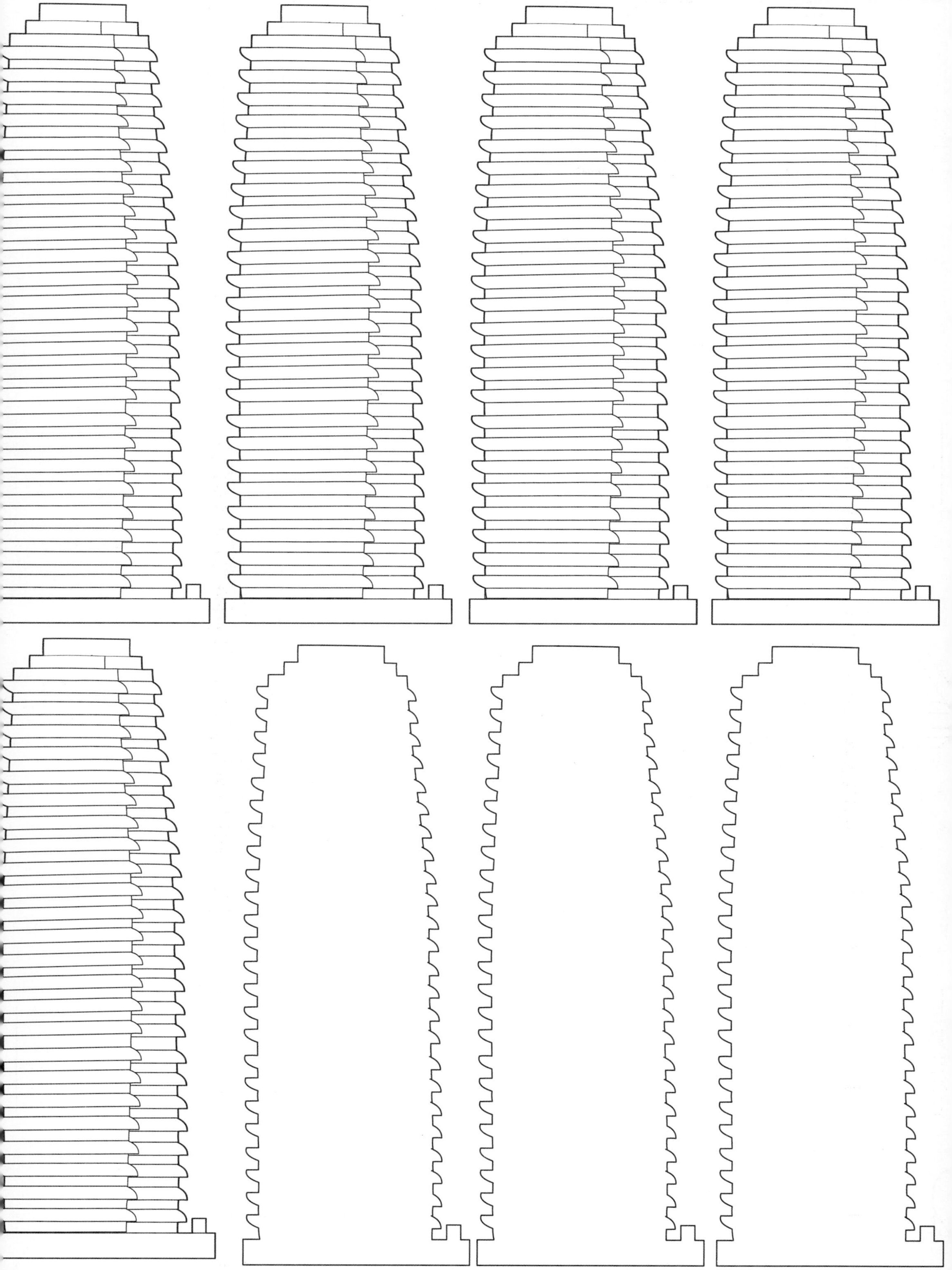

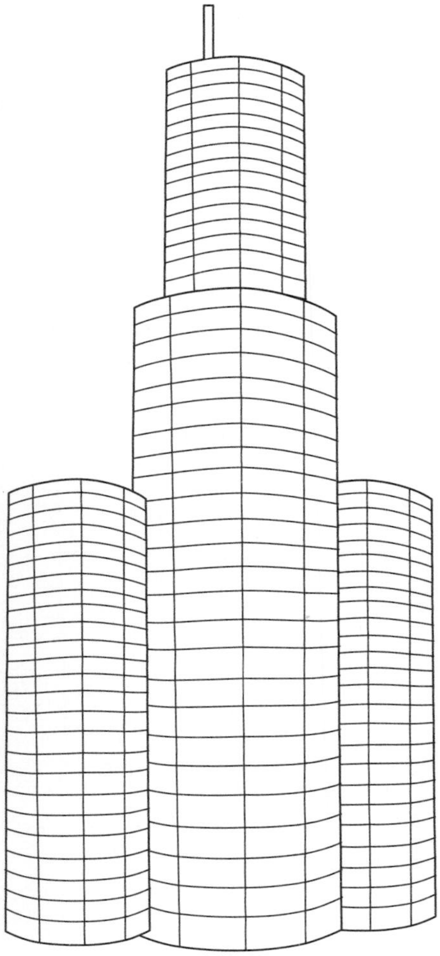
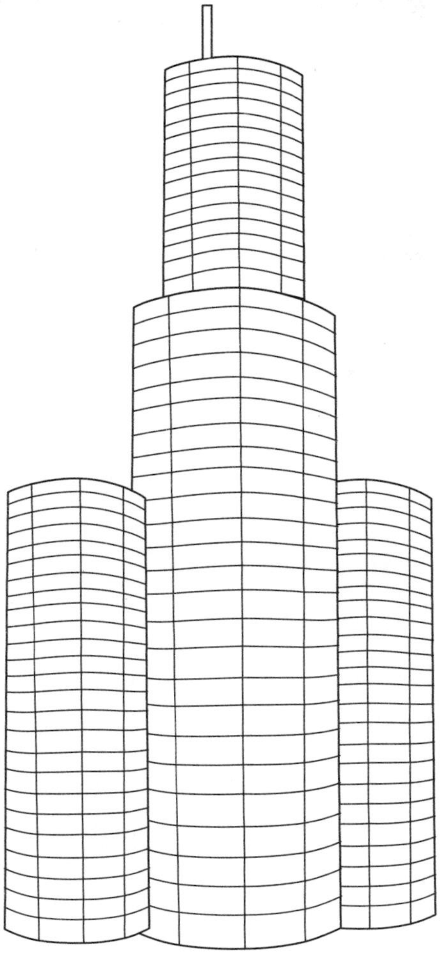
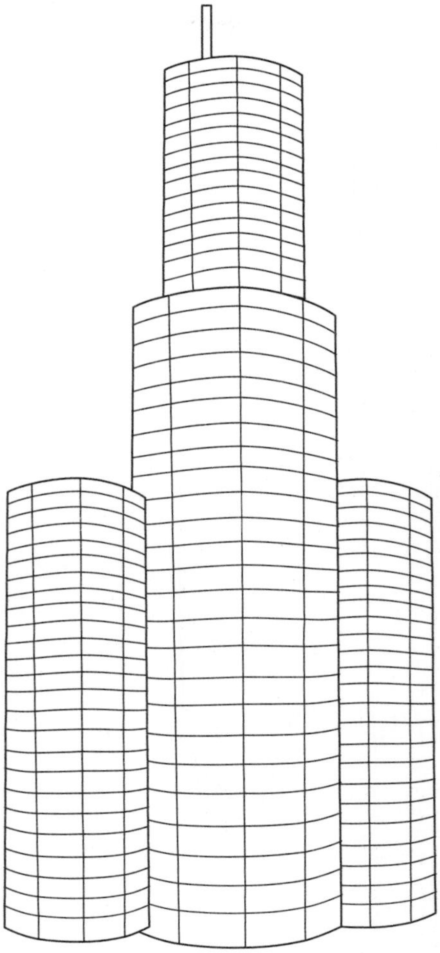
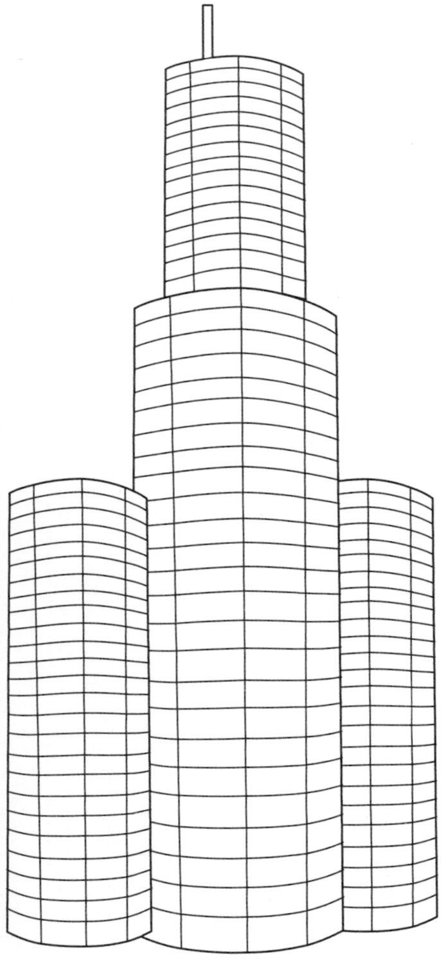
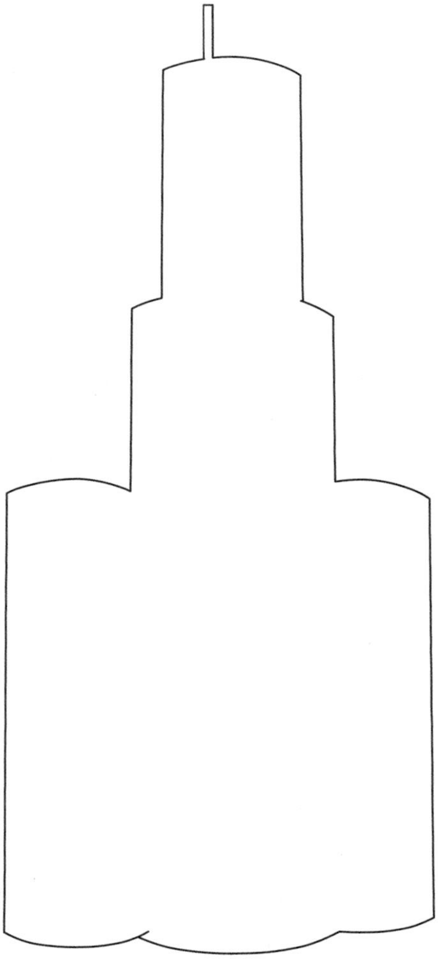
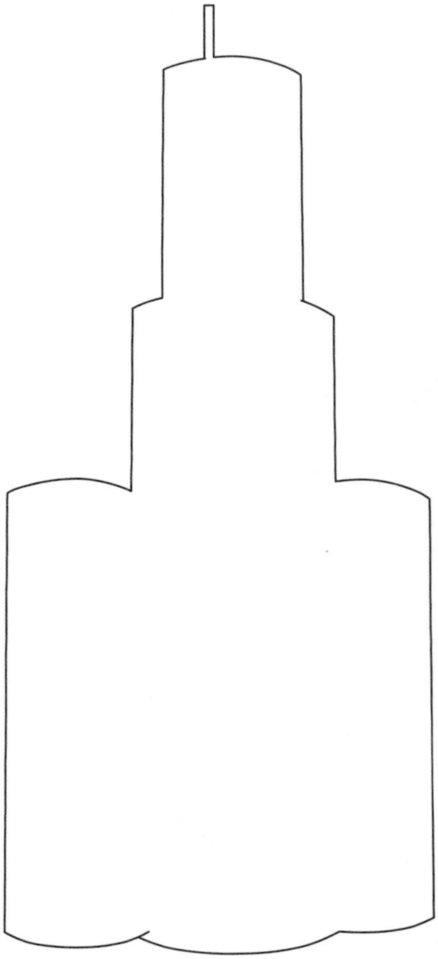

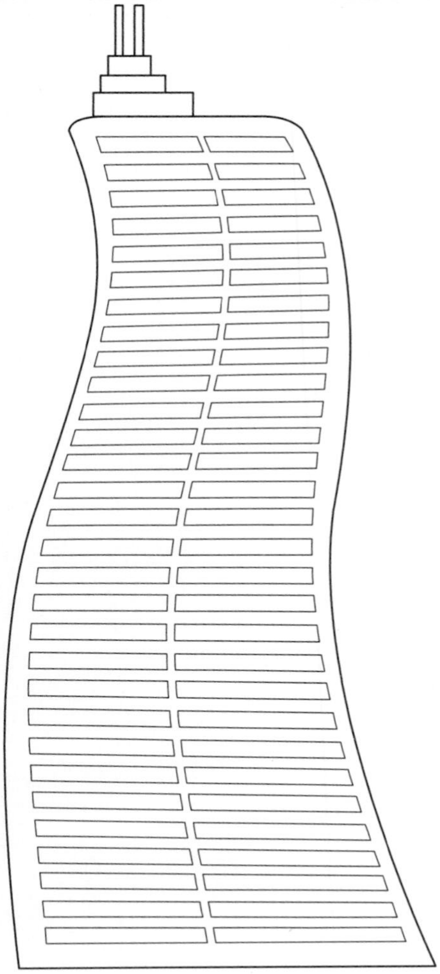
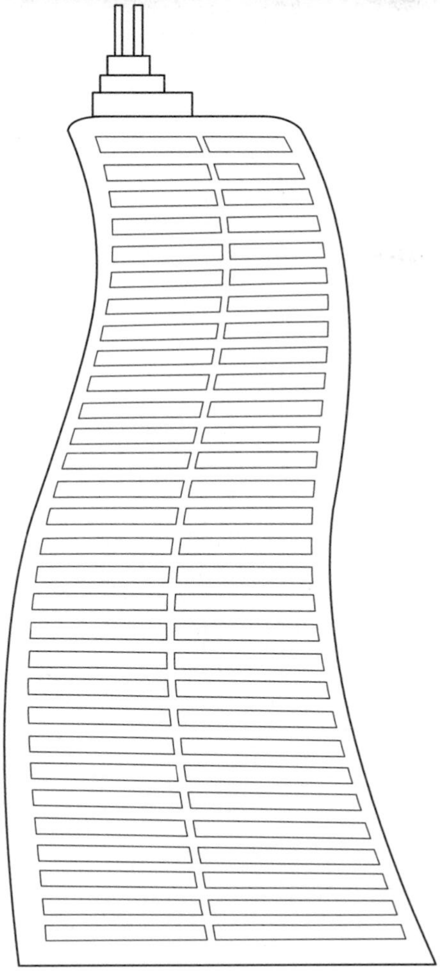
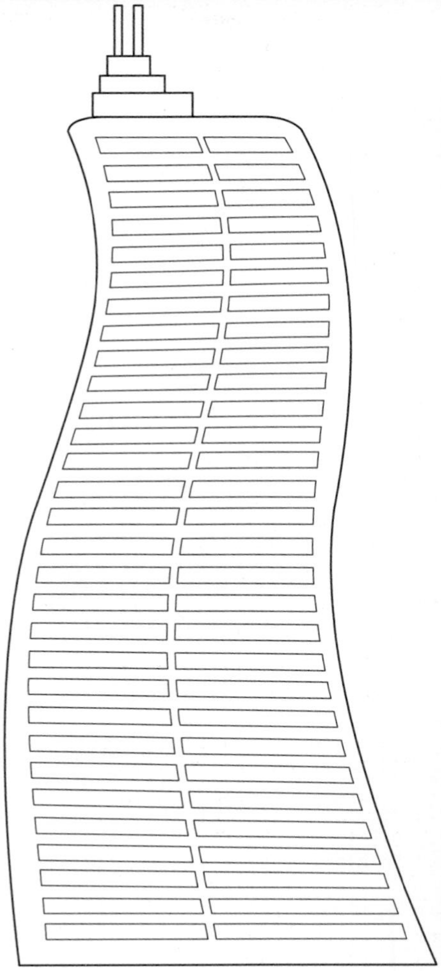
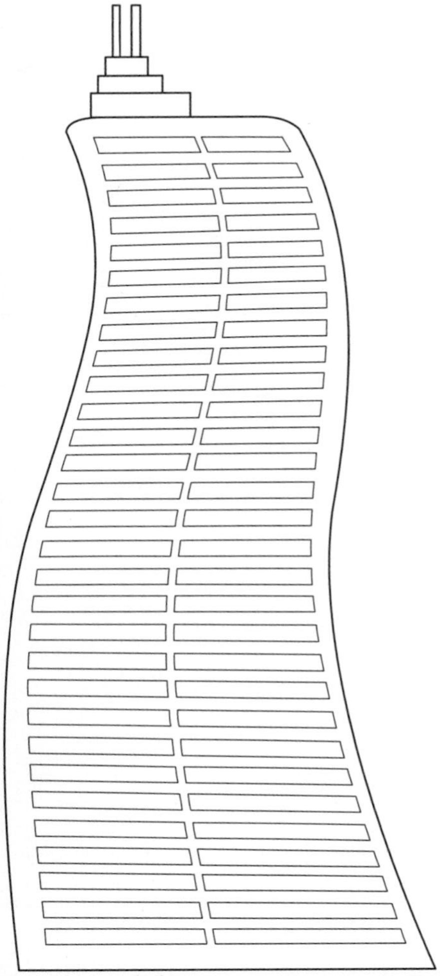
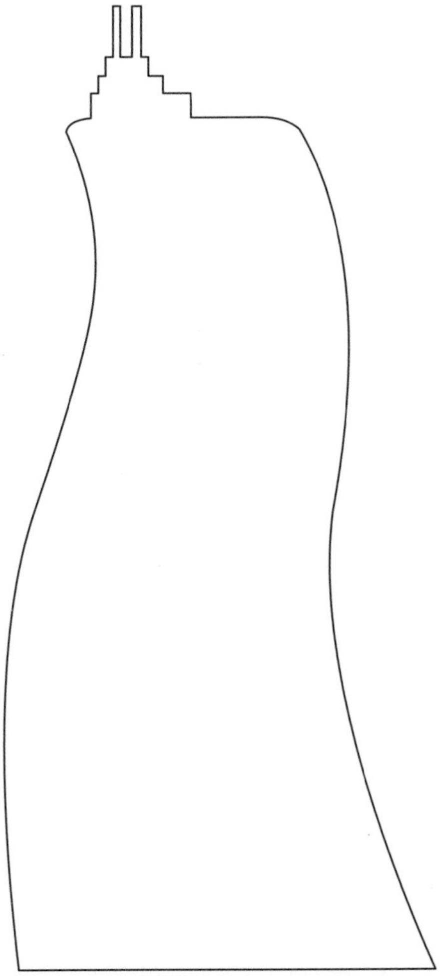
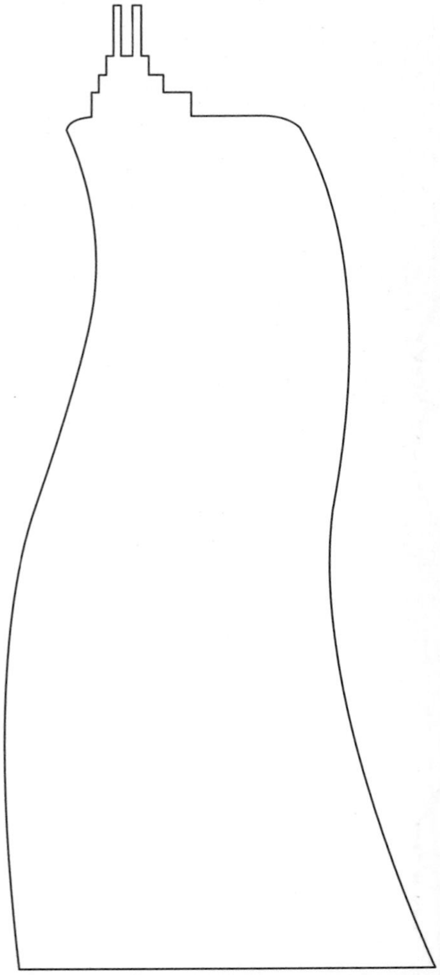

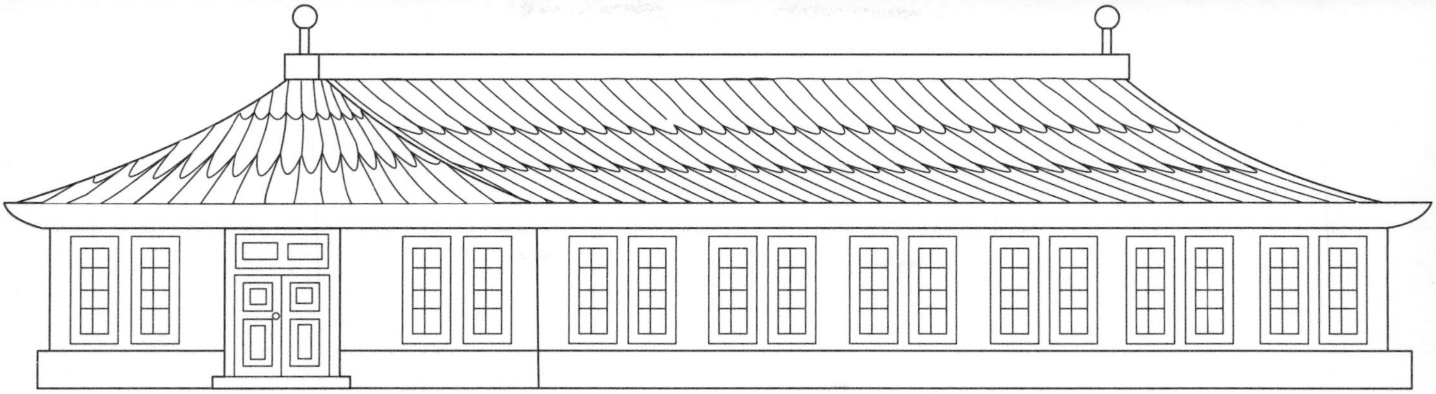

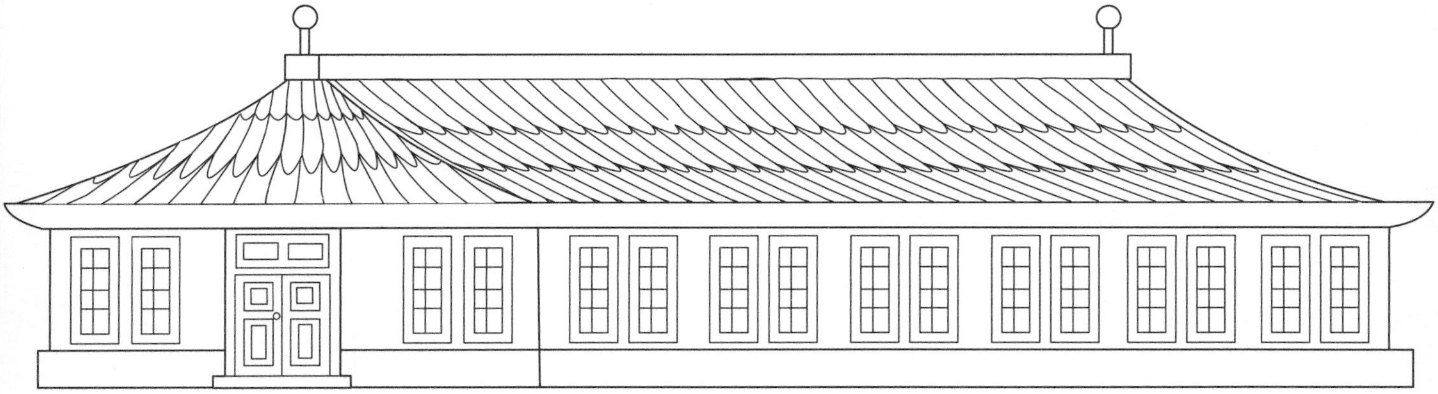

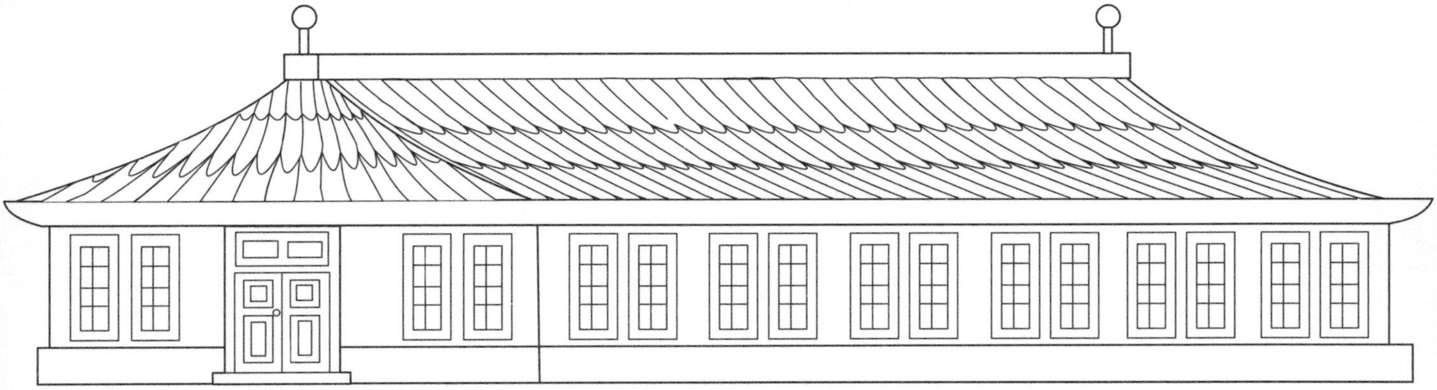

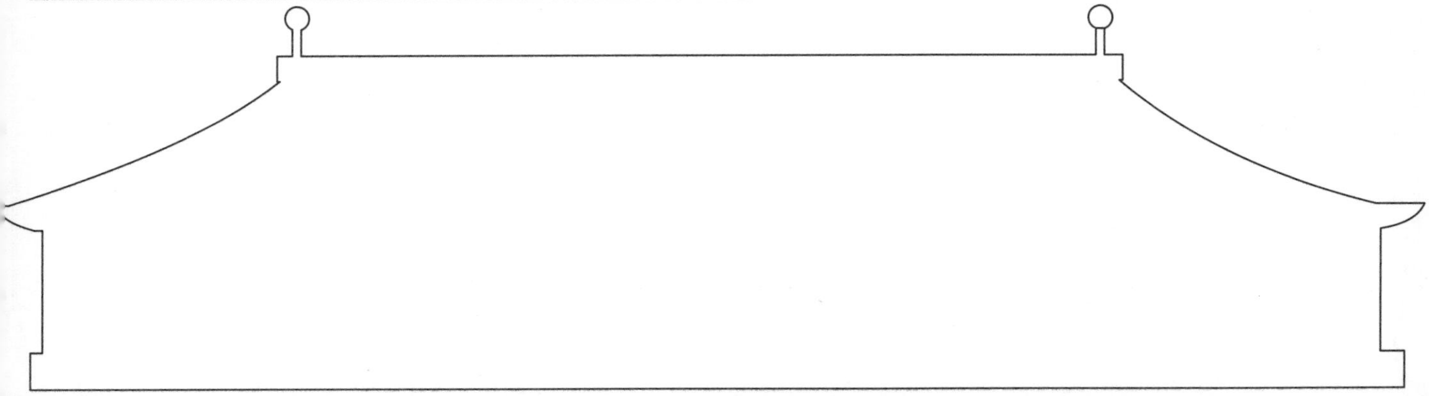

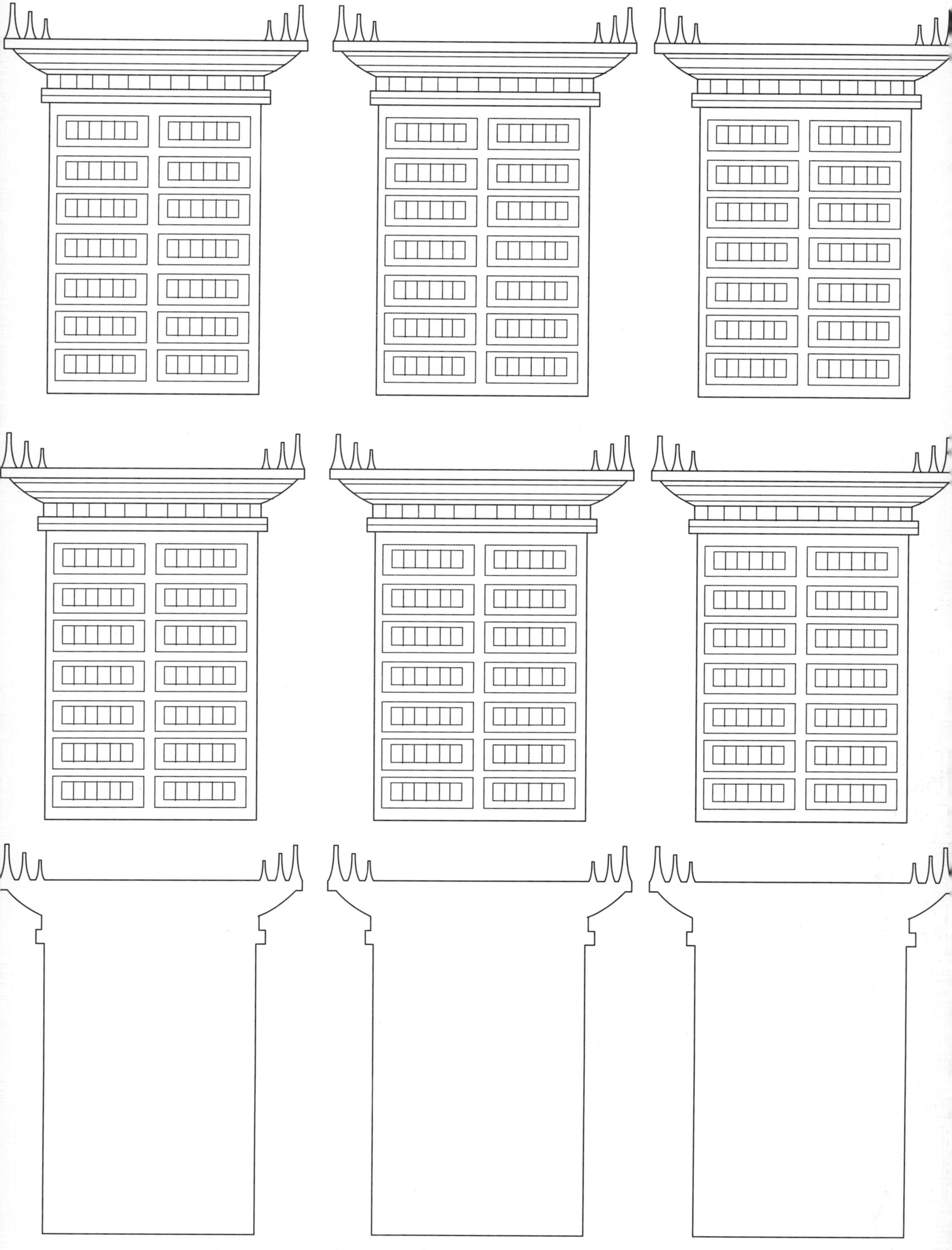

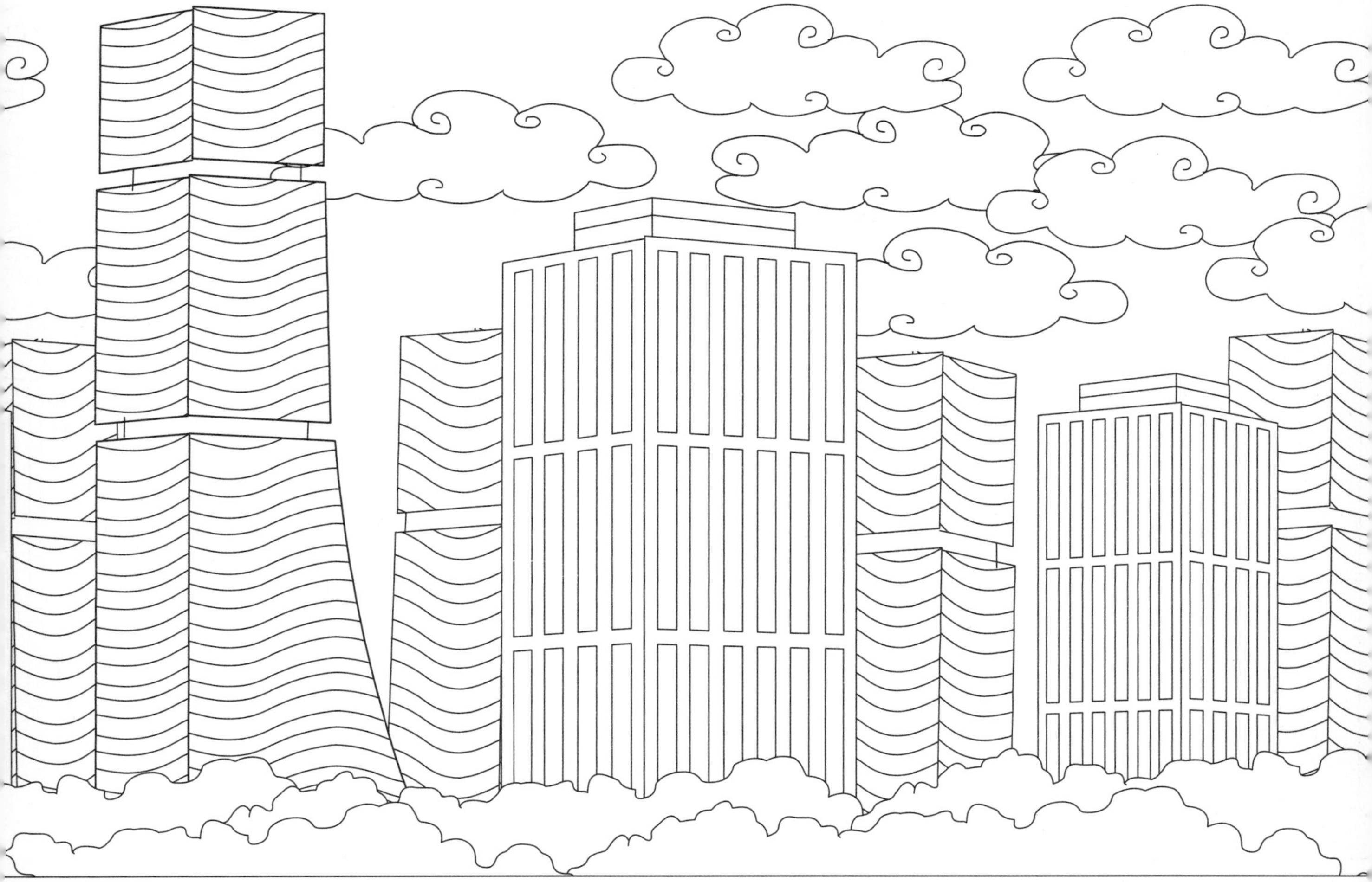

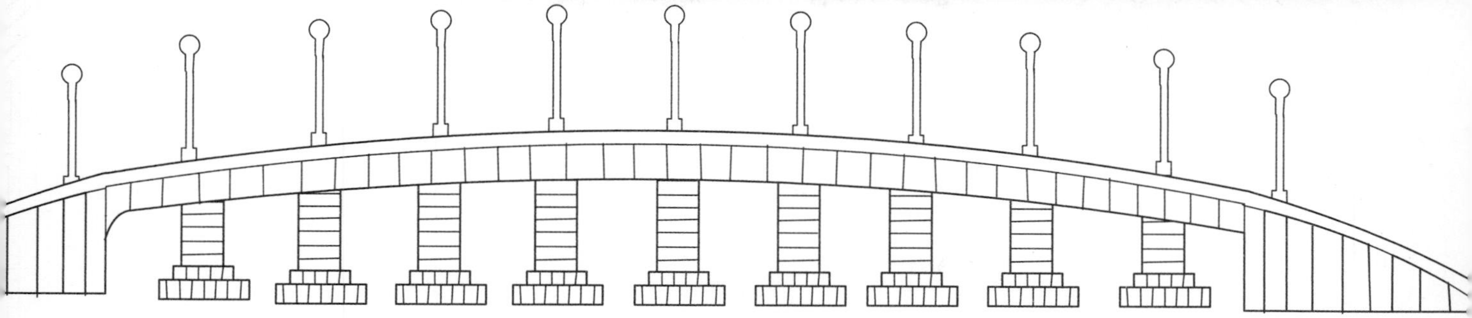
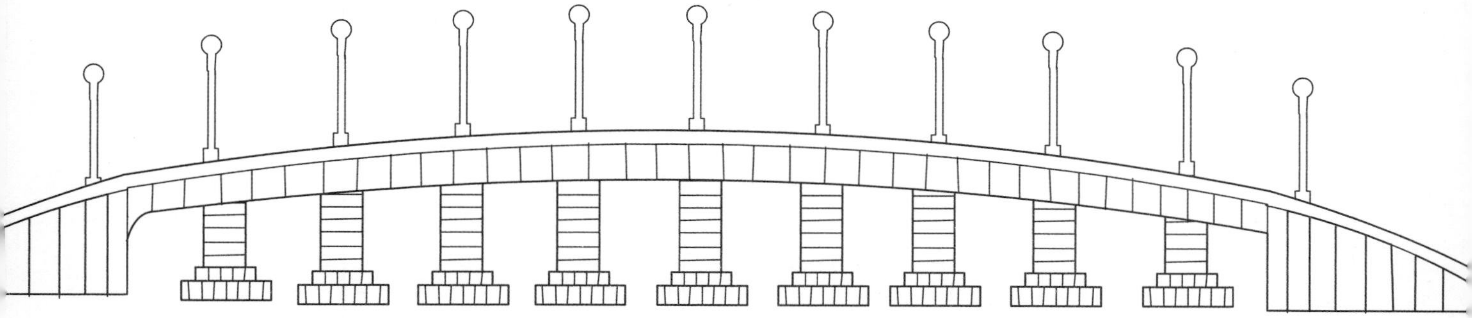
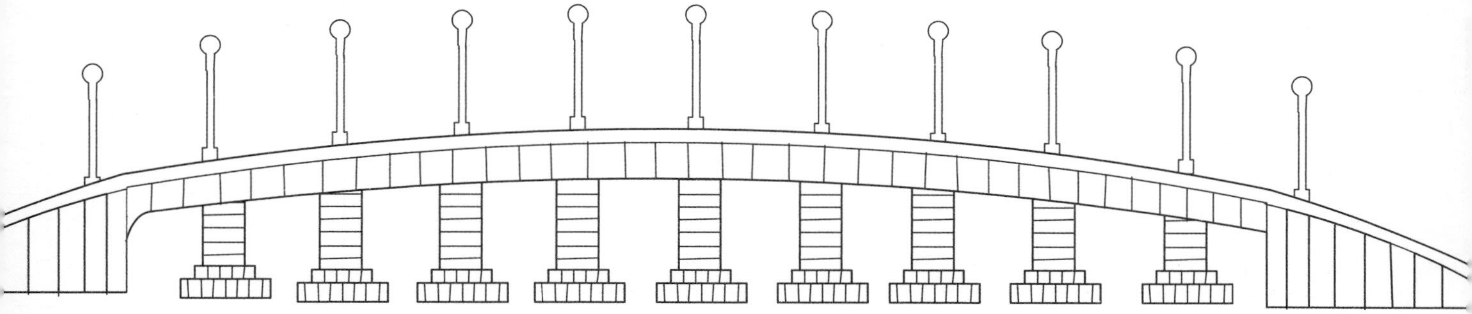
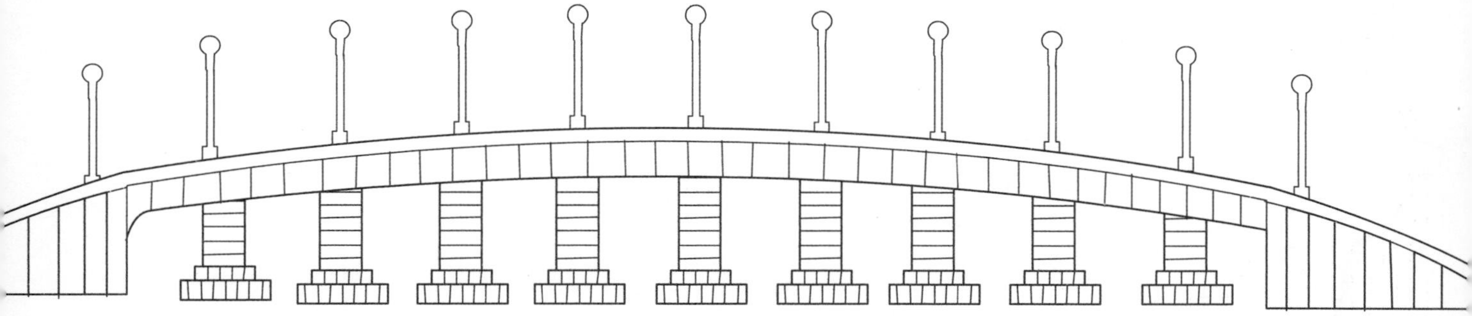
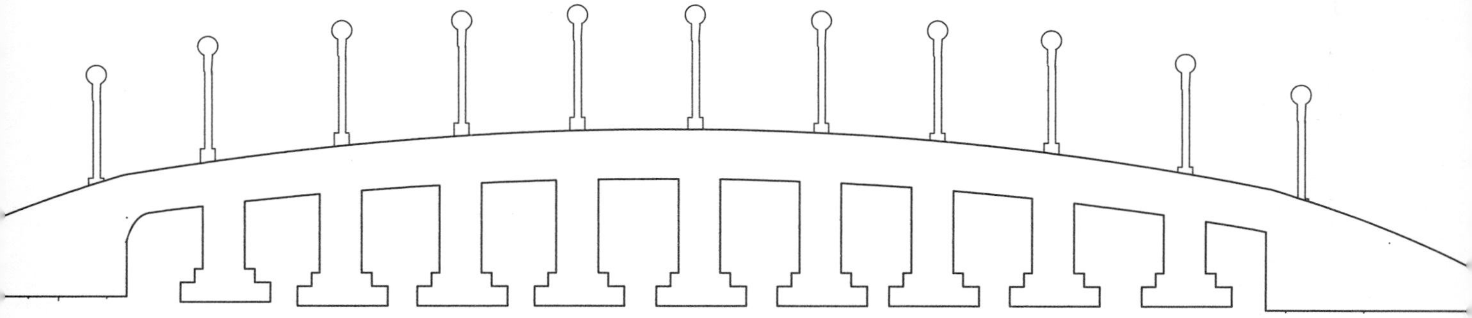
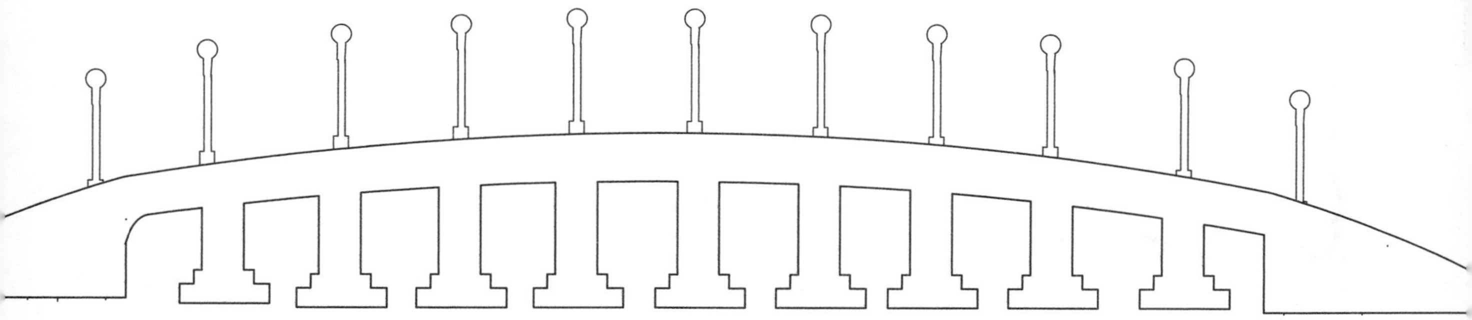

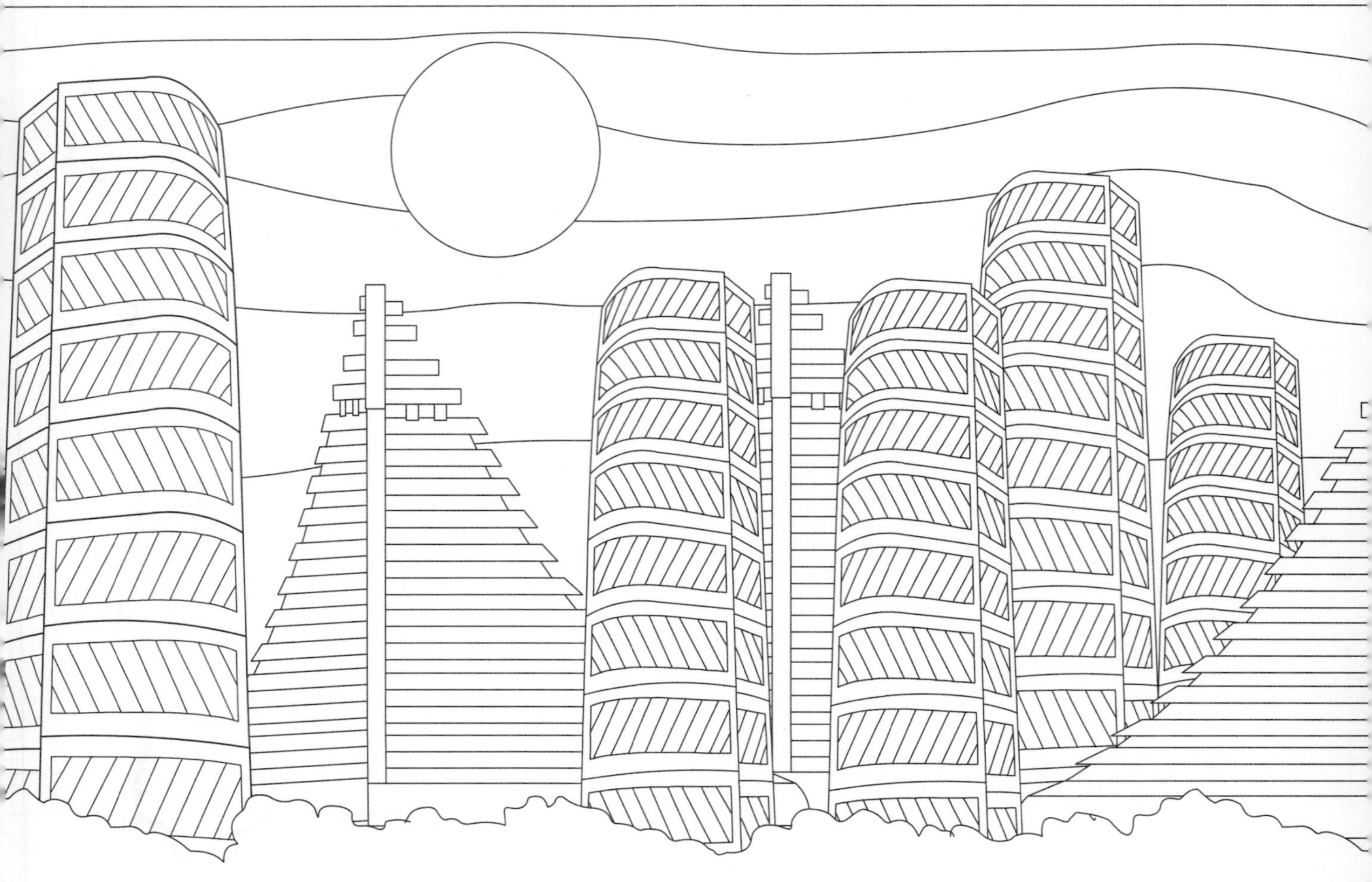

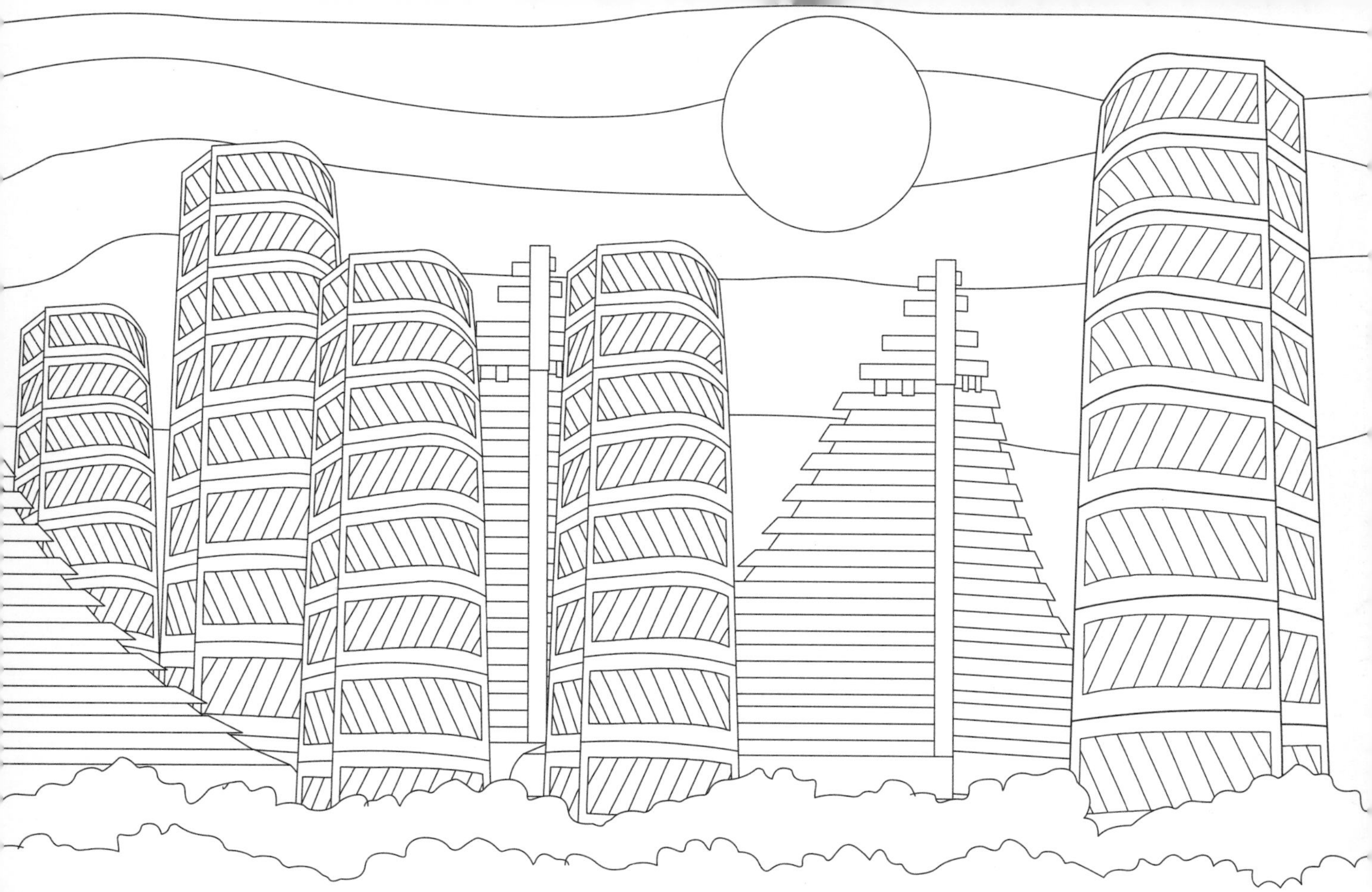